I0530615

# *It Makes Me Want To Cry When I Consider The Goodness of God*

## Volume I

# Susan Stem

Studio Griffin
A Publishing Company
www.studiogriffin.net

It Makes Me Want To Cry When I Consider The Goodness of God.
Copyright © 2024. Susan Stem

All Rights Reserved. Printed in the United States of America.
No part of this book may be used or reproduced in any manner whatsoever
without written permission except in the case of brief quotations embodied
in critical articles and reviews.

Scripture quotations taken from the Holy Bible, New International
Version®. Copyright © 1973, 1978, 1984 International Bible Society. Used
by permission of Zondervan. All rights reserved. The "NIV" and "New
International Version" trademarks are registered in the United States Patent
and Trademark Office by International Bible Society. Use of either
trademark requires the permission of International Bible Society.

Cover Design by Ruth E. Griffin/Studio Griffin

Cover Image by © Jimmy Brown

Photos used by author with permission.

First Edition

ISBN-13: 978-1-954818-46-0

Library of Congress Control Number: 2024909824

1 2 3 4 5 6 7 8 9 10

# DEDICATION

This book is dedicated first of all to Jesus because He is the reason that I have any God stories at all. He has been and continues to be the Lover of my soul, my Deliverer, my Redeemer, and He is the reason that I have thrived in my season of survival. Just as Shadrach, Meshach and Abenego came out of the fiery furnace not harmed in any way, nor was their hair singed, nor did their clothes smell like smoke, I, too, have not been harmed and have only grown and gotten closer to Jesus than ever before as I have experienced His lavish love through every fiery trial.

Jay, you have been such a huge part of God's redemption in my life. Being married to you is the most amazing and unbelievable blessing and we both know that only God could have brought us together. God spoke to me after my divorce, though He did not restore my first marriage that I had prayed fervently for, He would restore my life. God also spoke to you that He would do more than you could have ever dreamed or imagined, and He has truly done this. I am so thankful for your encouragement and support to enable me with time to write down the God stories in my life and proceed with publishing this book for others to benefit from hearing about God's intervention in my life. I will be forever grateful for your steady, faithful love and support for me to accomplish the desires of my heart.

Benjamin and John-Mark, you both are truly a gift from God. Together, we have experienced God's faithfulness and lavish love and provision through every difficult and delightful season. I am so thankful for the years I was able to stay at home with you and teach you in the ways of the Lord and I have been so blessed by the privilege to witness your growth and development into the young men that you are today.

Even today, I John 3:4 continues to be true in my life:

*I have no greater joy than when my sons are walking in the truth.*

I am so thankful also for the way that you, John-Mark, and Anna are training your daughter, Abigail, in the ways of the Lord.

Abigail, you are a true delight of my heart and life. God has so blessed our family with YOU! I pray that you will always love the Lord with all your heart, soul, mind, and strength. Through dedicating this book to you, I want to pass on a legacy to you of remembering and recording all the ways that God has worked in your life. I am sure you will go through many difficult and challenging times, but I pray that you will always believe and trust that God is God, He is good, and He only has good plans for your life. He never wants to harm you, but He will indeed use the hard times for good and to draw you into a closer relationship with Him if you are willing. I pray you have a personal relationship with Jesus and grow stronger through every day of your life. You will always be in my prayers for as long as I live.

To my true friends who provided love, encouragement, provision, truth, and life support to me when I could barely breathe in the fiery trials, I will be eternally grateful to you. I know that God placed you in my life for these times, and I am not sure that I would have survived without your continuing intervention and love in my life. I am so thankful for all the ways that you comforted me, spurred me on to love and good deeds with truth, powerful word pictures, notes of encouragement, outlets for restful getaways and especially always pointing me to Jesus.

# CONTENTS

# FOREWORD

For quite a while, God has impressed on me the need to write down all the ways He has blessed and intervened in my life. Then in 2020, God emphatically said, "NOW is the time to write."

I could not even begin to share all the God stories in my life, but this is my attempt to record just a fraction of all of His faithfulness in my life. Everything you read is actual events. These God moments are part of my story, but our God is the same and He will do the same for you as He has for me. Trust and obey His voice and seek Him on behalf of your situation and He will be sure to show Himself mighty on your behalf. Always remember as well that even though God does not grant your every request as you have asked, His ways and thoughts are so much higher than ours and if He says, "No," or "Wait," there is a higher purpose that He has planned for your life. Trust Him and the process that He uses to conform us to His image and make us more like Him. He loves you so much and only has your good in mind and His glory.

I believe that God wants me to share these stories to encourage others in their journey and remind them of the faithfulness of God.

I love the following verses because it sums up how God allows us to go through trials with His comfort and then we can comfort others as they go through similar things. Ultimately, the purpose is to draw all of us into a closer relationship with Jesus. Please pray as you read these verses slowly and carefully; and ask God to open up the eyes of your understanding, so that you will be able to comprehend all that God has for you.

*Praise be to the God and Father of our Lord Jesus Christ, the Father of compassion and the God of all comfort, who comforts us in all our troubles, so that we can comfort those in any trouble with the comfort we ourselves receive from God. For just as we share abundantly in the sufferings of Christ, so also our comfort abounds through Christ. If we are distressed, it is for your comfort and salvation; if we are comforted, it is for your comfort, which produces in you patient endurance of the same sufferings we suffer. And our hope for you is firm because we know that just as you share in our sufferings, so also you share in our comfort. We do not want you to be uninformed, brothers and sisters,[a] about the troubles we experienced in the province of Asia. We were under great pressure, far beyond our ability to endure, so that we despaired of life itself. Indeed, we felt we had received the sentence of death. But this happened that we might not rely on ourselves but on God, who raises the dead. He has delivered us from such a deadly peril, and he will deliver us again. On him we have set our hope that he will continue to deliver us, as you help us by your prayers. Then many will give thanks on our behalf for the gracious favor granted us in answer to the prayers of many. 2 Corinthians 1:3-11*

*Susan Stem*

# WELL, I WOKE UP THIS MORNING FEELING FINE!

O h, how I love it when God wakes me up with a song in my heart and mind. This is an old song entitled, 'Feeling Mighty Fine' by the Statler Brothers that I have not heard for years, yet God reminded me of recently:

*Well, I'm feeling mighty fine I've got heaven on my mind*
*Don't you know I want to go where the milk and honey flow*
*There's a light that always shines down inside this heart of mine*
*I've got heaven on my mind and I'm feeling mighty fine*

I remember growing up, my dad, mom, me and my three sisters would gather around the piano and sing this and many other songs together. I don't know if I really appreciated those times during my youth, but today they are fond memories of my family singing praises to Jesus together. I am so thankful my parents instilled godly truths in my heart and were always faithful to take me to church and youth activities; and it is because of them that I have such a personal relationship with Jesus today.

Since accepting Jesus into my life at an early age, I have always tried to please Him, but I realize now that I used to often just ask Him to bless my plans. Later, in my early adult life while navigating some very painful experiences, I began to seek God's will and agenda for my life. My dear friend, Marsha, once told me, "Obey Jesus, moment by moment," which has been a life-changing truth.

I love Jeremiah 29:11 which states,

> *For I know the plans I have for you, declares the Lord, plans to prosper you and not to harm you, plans to give you hope and a future.*

Also, Proverbs 3:5-6 says,

> *Trust in the Lord with all your heart, and lean not on your own understanding. In all your ways acknowledge Him and He will direct your paths.*

As for me, I am continuing to learn to trust and obey Him. As I continue to grow, I can testify that my life has truly become quite an adventure with Captain Jesus at the helm of my life.

# MY DULL, BORING ROUTINE LIFE

Yes, I am one of the fortunate ones to have grown up in a dull, boring, routine life, but I wasn't always appreciative of this. I grew up in the days when we ate together as a family every night and rarely went out to eat at a restaurant. We had chores, including working in the garden, pulling weeds, preparing meals together and cleaning up afterwards by washing all the dishes by hand. When we wanted to play, my sisters and friends went outside, and we played badminton and kickball; and climbed trees. We read lots of books and had early morning Bible studies with mom during the summers.

My parents always made homemade baked goods and never bought individually wrapped snacks. We picked berries with my dad and then made pies, jams, and jellies. Since we had a big garden, summer evenings always included shelling peas, snapping beans, shucking corn, cutting up tomatoes, cooking squash, and cutting up asparagus. While canning the vegetables, my job as the youngest usually consisted of watching the cooker build up pressure. Our house was always filled with aromas of fresh vegetables as they were being prepared for canning or freezing. The smell of corn was my favorite. Our basement was converted into a corn processing plant. First, it was blanched, then it had to be cooled before we all got a knife and began cutting it off the cob. It was quite a process with the entire family participating.

On Sundays, we always went to church in the morning and evening; and on Wednesdays, we went in the evenings, and this was never up for discussion. We could always count on dad to make rolled oats every Sunday morning, whether we wanted them or not.

We picked pears off the tree and all the mushy ones that fell off and tried to avoid getting stung by the bees. We watched evening primrose flowers open up before our very eyes with our family and neighbors. We caught lightning bugs and kept them in plain old jars, not fancy containers. We played hide-and-seek outdoors and freeze tag. I always had a love for our cats, and we always seemed to acquire additional strays that took up residence at our home. We had picnics on almost every holiday instead of going on elaborate vacations like other families. We visited our uncle's farm and helped them bale hay, milk the cows, and carry it to the milk house during the summers.

Our TV broke and my dad decided we had more quality family time without it, so it was never repaired. We played lots of games together as a family. My dad loved to cook, and he often made homemade fudge and rice pudding.

On hot summer nights, my three sisters and I made our way downstairs to sleep, since the only air conditioning we owned was box fans placed in our windows.

While I was growing up, I was always wishing for more excitement and certainly did not appreciate the life my parents provided for me. Today, I look back and thank God for the value of a stable home, loving parents who provided healthy foods to help my body grow strong (even though I was a very picky eater), taught me the benefit of work and the satisfaction it can bring, taught me about how things grow, ate together as a family, played games together, and worshipped Jesus together.

My family life may not have been the most exciting, but I am thankful for all their loving support and exposing me to the love of Jesus. I am so thankful for growing up in a home where Proverbs 22:6 (*Train up a child in the way he should go; even when he is old, he will not depart from it*) was put into practice. This has provided me with a solid foundation with eternal dividends and one that has been passed onto my sons.

# SPURRED BY THE SEARS TELEMARKETER

When I became a single mom, life was challenging, especially financially. God continually blessed me and provided what we needed but there was not much left by the end of the month.

One day, I received one of those calls from a telemarketer wanting me to purchase something from Sears. I was definitely not in the place to purchase anything, but I was patient with him as he proceeded. When I got a chance to speak, I let this telemarketer named Jesse know about my current situation of being newly separated with two young sons, and no income. He immediately changed hats and became a messenger from Jesus that day. He told me that he was a Christian and that this crisis would make me stronger. He proceeded to tell me about his co-worker who he said was spiritually anointed and he wanted her to pray for me. He put her on the phone, and she prayed for me. WOW! What an encouragement it was to me. Sears called to solicit for business and instead was used as a conduit of Jesus' love and blessing to me that day.

I am sure that each of us have had struggles in our lives God has helped us overcome and still have challenges we deal with every day. Let's remember to seize opportunities to encourage others in their difficulties.

*Let us consider how we may spur one another on toward love and good deeds. Let us encourage one another and all the more you as you see the Day approaching. Hebrew 10:24-25b*

*Let us not become weary in doing good, for at the proper time, we will reap a harvest IF we do not give up.* Galatians 6:9

So, next time you meet a stranger, receive a call from a telemarketer, acquaintance or just a friend, be a conduit of God's love and encourage them. You will never know the potential impact and huge difference it could make in their life.

# THE ROPE OF HOPE

My dear friend, Karen has been such a blessing to my life. We have had many parallel life experiences and as a result, we have been able to share hope and comfort back and forth to each other.

We met each other one Sunday morning in our apartment building. We were preparing to leave for church, and we agreed to ride together. On the way there she shared how she had just moved there from Ohio, was terribly homesick, had no friends there, and to top it off, her closet fell down under the weight of all her clothes that morning. After church, we shared lunch together and helped get her closet fixed. We quickly became kindred spirits.

We were both from Ohio and had hearts to serve the Lord which led us to the Word of Life ministry. We began dating 2 guys that were roommates at the Bible Institute and we had lots of fun on our double dates. This led to engagements and soon weddings just a month apart. We were very happy, and both became pregnant at the same time. We each had 2 children that are the same age. We both experienced a miscarriage. We both had marriages that ended not as we had planned, but we both held onto Jesus through it all and we became stronger women as a result. We both went back to school and now have bachelor's degrees. We both are now remarried to wonderful godly men and are excited about the rest of the chapters in our lives.

During one of my hard seasons that Karen had already walked through, she encouraged me by sending me a care package that included the following: a music CD, bath gels, a candle, calming specialty teas, two fun videos to make me laugh and a card to remind me to hold onto the rope of hope and that I would survive that difficult time. She was God's conduit of love reminding me that God was the Lover of my soul and He had not forgotten about my needs.

Karen has had one additional very hard chapter in her life, which I am thus far not acquainted with. She was blessed with a 3rd child who was an extra special blessing amidst one of her very painful seasons. Andy was one of the most loving sons but after 20 short years Jesus carried him to Heaven. I cannot imagine the deep loss that she has lived through, but I can see that Jesus has also carried her through this dark time. I am thankful for those who have been able to comfort her that have already experienced this and received God's comfort.

*Praise be to the God who comforts us in all our troubles, so that we can comfort those in any trouble with the comfort we ourselves have received from God. For just as the sufferings of Christ flow over into our lives, so also through Christ our comfort overflows. But this happened that we might not rely on ourselves but on God. 2 Corinthians 1:3-5, 9*

I am so thankful for the dear friends God has placed in my life and for the Holy Spirit to bring comfort to us. Rely on HIM and be willing to be a conduit of His love and extend the rope of hope to those around you who need HIS comfort and encouragement.

# STEAK AND POTATOES

The years 2002 and 2003 taught me to pray like I have never prayed before. My desperation dropped me to my knees, and I became very specific and intentional about my prayer list. I prayed for the biggest needs to the smallest of desires. God showed up in so many amazing ways and He demonstrated time after time, that...

*He is able to do more than we could ever ask or imagine, according to His power that is at work within us and He is worthy of all glory. Ephesians 3:20-21*

This particular time I was praying for potatoes, but I had not shared this need with anyone else. God definitely heard my prayer for very soon I was given potatoes in every form and fashion. First, I went to a Valentine's dinner with our homeschool group and my friend Ginny sent me home with all the leftover delicious twice-baked potatoes she had made. God even had them prepared gourmet style. Second, my friend Jimmy filled my van with boxes of food donated by Wellspring for myself and Teen Valley Ranch which included potatoes. Third, one of my neighbors, Mark, invited me to pick up the leftovers from the Senior Valentine's dinner which included lots of boiled potatoes already cooked and prepared for me. Finally, another neighbor, Gwen dropped off several bags of potatoes as she had extra.

Shortly after all the potatoes began piling up at my home, I was invited to a ladies' prayer seminar with my friend, Anita. The speaker shared that prayer does several things. Prayer reminds us that God is in sovereign control. It reveals God's will, it promotes growth and an intimate relationship with Jesus, and it helps us to focus God's power upon a specific need. While sitting at the table

I shared God's blessings and provision with all the potatoes. Upon hearing this story, a lady spoke up and said, "You might want to start praying for steak instead of potatoes."

We all laughed but hopefully we all learned that God wants to bless us, and we should never just settle for the little things and scraps from the King's table. God has a banquet table He is preparing for us, so be bold in your prayers.

Malachi 3:10b says,

> *God says, test me in this and see if I will not throw open the floodgates of heaven and pour you out so much blessing that you will not have enough room for it.*

Psalms 81:10 also says,

> *Open your mouths wide and I will fill it.*

So, in your times of need, begin to pray boldly, obey God's truths, and trust Him to bless you beyond your wildest dreams and never settle for just the scraps from the King's table.

# THE PROPHET

I grew up in a very conservative Christian home and attended a Baptist church. After graduation, I attended Word of Life Bible Institute which expanded my Christian experiences. As an adult, I attended a non-denominational church, and I began to cultivate friendships with those of a more charismatic background. I also visited a Spirit-filled Messianic Jewish church which I thoroughly enjoyed witnessing many of the Jewish traditions that they practiced. Kissing the Torah always touched my heart as they showed such honor and reverence for God's Holy word. I also met many friends while homeschooling who also embraced spirit-filled experiences. Though I was not familiar with many of these practices, I began learning that God ministered to His children in more ways than I had ever realized.

One of these ways was when I attended the funeral of my dear friend, Michelle Rogers. She had developed cancer and though she prayed and had faith that God was going to heal her, God chose to heal her in Heaven instead of on earth. Before she passed, I had many sweet times with her in her home as well as in the hospital. One of my fondest memories was the time that we sang together during a very painful day for her. She continued to praise Jesus every step of the way and she was a beautiful example to me of faithfulness to her Lord.

On the day of her funeral, while I was visiting with her family and friends, something very unusual happened to me that still amazes me today. I did not know anyone in the room except the friend I came with, but one of the gentlemen there stood up in the room and spoke directly to me. He told me he was a prophet and that he had been watching me. He said there was something very special about me and God wanted me to know that He had had

His hand on me for all of my life. He had protected me from many things and had something very special in store for me.

I was quite taken back by this, but at the same time, I was honored and felt very blessed. I received these words and tucked them in my heart.

Over the years, when I have pondered this, God has made me aware of times that He had been protecting and sheltering me from harm. One of the times was when I was in sixth grade and had not been invited to a slumber party with all the popular girls. I felt left out until I learned that they had all gone streaking down the road and then I felt relieved because I would not have been comfortable doing that. Now, I can see that God was not setting me aside, but rather setting me apart for His purposes and guarding me so that I would not be in harm's way.

Another time when I was at a friend's house for a party, and they decided to have a seance in their basement. Well, I knew that was messing with Satan which scared me. God gave me the courage to sit with her parents upstairs until it was over. God again protected me by giving me the strength to stand up for what I believed and not take part of evil.

In the Bible, it states that the proof of a true prophet is that his words come true (Deuteronomy 18:22). Well, today I am confident that God truly has had His hand on my life and has blessed me over and over. I can also see how in the midst of all the hard, painful seasons of my life, He has transformed me through it all. I did not see God's hand at the time, but now, I can see His fingerprints all over my life and I am so thankful for Philippians 1:6 which says we can...

*Be confident of this, that he who began a good work in you will carry it on to completion until the day of Christ Jesus.*

# THE BIRTHDAY GIFT
# I DIDN'T WANT

I sold my house in 2016 but the house I wanted to buy sold before I could purchase it which placed me in quite a predicament. I was not sure where I should live or what God had in mind for me, but I was praying and believed God would direct my path.

During that time, I received a call from my friends, Steve and Sharon, and they offered me the chance to stay in their beautiful and empty townhome until I could find a place. I was amazed at God's timing and provision and was so grateful. I was steadily looking for another home but did not find anything. Finally, about ten months later, I moved to my dear friend Anne's home after she went to be with Jesus. I knew that her house was up for sale, but her daughters were allowing me to rent it until it sold. At first, I was so worried it would sell that I was not even able to enjoy the beautiful home that God had once again provided for me. One day in early April 2017 during my Bible study time, God led me to the verse in Acts 17:26b which reads:

> He (God) determined the times set for them and the exact places where they should live.

WOW! I wrote in my Bible next to the verse, "What a comfort this reminder was to me that God is in charge, and He is aware of my situation." From that day on, I was full of confidence and peace that God wanted me to enjoy this home and would not allow the house to sell until I had found another home.

Just days later on my birthday, April 23, 2017, while I was enjoying lunch with my sons, I received a phone call. Anne's daughter, Luanne, called to let me know that they had accepted a cash offer on the house, and they would be closing in May, so I would need to move out by the end of May. I hung up the phone and tears began to roll down my face. I thought, what a birthday gift to be homeless. I tried to enjoy the rest of the meal, but I was stricken with fear and worry. Later that day, Luanne called me back to let me know of a rental house that was newly renovated and ready for occupancy.

The next morning, as I was preparing to go see it, I told God, "I sure know how foster kids feel!"

God quickly responded to me, "Oh no you do not. You have a job and the means to purchase a house today if you choose to."

I quickly understood God's response and thanked Him for His provision. I signed the rental contract later that day and realized that God had provided a place for me the same day He allowed the first one to sell.

Having to move again was truly a gift that I did not want at first. At the time, I could not see what God was working out on my behalf. Now, I can see that God had everything in order and His timing was perfect. If the house had sold later, I would have missed the rental home which provided everything I needed for the next two years until He gave me the biggest surprise of all: an amazing husband and a beautiful brick home.

# WAYS PAST FINDING OUT

For my thoughts are not your thoughts, neither are your ways my ways, saith the LORD. For as the heavens are higher than the earth, so are my ways higher than your ways, and my thoughts than your thoughts. Isaiah 55:8-9

O the depth of the riches both of the wisdom and knowledge of God! How unsearchable are his judgments, and his ways past finding out! Romans 11:33

God woke me up one morning reminding me that His ways are past finding out in particular regarding a seed. A seed can be stored for years without water or light. Yet, if placed in conditions that are conducive to growth, it will begin to sprout and demonstrate signs of life. I cannot comprehend how it can remain viable through the years without any visible evidence.

I also ponder the human body and how it is such an incredible piece of machinery that works seemingly all by itself, yet we know that there is an amazing Creator who has not missed one thing we need.

I am 56 years old, and my heart has been beating 60-100 beats per minute and has not so far had one problem. My eyes have lubrication which keeps my eyes from being dry and excruciatingly painful. All the wounds, scrapes and cuts I have gotten through my life have all healed without any help from me. My intestinal system breaks my food down to feed every cell in my body and then elimination happens to dispose of what is left. My brain tells my lungs to breathe in and out without any assistance from me. Even as I sit here typing and processing what I need to write, God is allowing my brain to communicate to my fingers to type it out. As a nurse, when I consider the amazing body that we have, I just have to praise the Lord.

Let's consider nature and the amazing things God has created. I learned in Biology that there are actually male and female components of a pine tree. They are strategically located on the tree—the spores are located above the pinecones, so that it will filter down and fertilize the female part.

Consider all the variety of foods God has created for us to enjoy: strawberries, blueberries, kiwi, cantaloupe, avocado, and list goes on and on.

Now, onto the beautiful intricate flowers that are so different but all so beautiful. From the common dandelion to the delicate orchids. He could have made just one kind but obviously HE loves variety and wants us to enjoy them.

Consider all the saltwater fish in the oceans that have some of the most exquisite colors and designs and most are always hidden from the observing eye as well as all the precious gems and metals concealed in the ground.

When I consider all God's creation and yet He takes time to personally wake me up each morning without an alarm clock, I am in complete awe of His amazing ways. He has proven over and over to me how much He loves me and wants to bless me. I hope that you have a personal relationship with HIM and enjoy His majestic creation.

# SPARRING WITH THE ENEMY

Back in 2002, Pastor Lee, a dear friend of our family, had begun providing counseling to support my sons after I became a single mom. He was offering that male role model they desperately needed which was a direct answer to my prayers. God took it to a greater level when Pastor Lee began providing karate lessons for them to give them a physical outlet for their stress. I was completely overwhelmed with God's provision first for the counseling and mentor relationship and then his sincere desire to invest into my son's hearts and lives.

As my sons continued to accomplish new levels in karate, it became more intense and required more energy and effort. Before each karate match, they had to put on all the sparring gear to protect themselves. It was challenging for them to learn to fight and be on guard to defend themselves while their opponent was continually looking where to strike next.

Many years have passed since then and we are not doing karate in a dojo, but we are definitely in a battle where the enemy is looking for a way to destroy us.

I Peter 5:8 says it best,

> Be self-controlled and alert. Your enemy the devil prowls around like a roaring lion looking for someone to devour. Resist him, standing firm in your faith, because you know that your brothers throughout the world are undergoing the same kind of sufferings.

Back then, it was hard to watch my sons get knocked around by their opponent, and today it is even harder to watch the enemy of their souls try to steal, kill, and destroy them. We as moms must remain vigilant in prayer for our children and ourselves. Remember to dress ourselves in the whole armor of God, just as my sons had to put on all the sparring gear, so that we can stand in the evil day and overcome the evil one (Ephesians 6:10-18).

# MY LEATHER COAT

2002 was a very stressful year for me and my sons. I became a single mom with no income, no savings, and no human resources to depend upon. It was during this season of my life I truly learned what an awesome Provider Jesus is. I was on my knees for my every need, desperately crying out to Him for my sons and myself. It was at the end of one of these prayers, I tagged on something that I personally wanted. My prayer ended something like this, "And God thank you for hearing my prayer and lastly, now, this is not a need, just a want, but I would really appreciate it if You would provide me with a leather coat. It's okay if you don't because you are still good and you are God. Thanks in advance. Amen." That was on a Monday.

On Thursday, our homeschool group met and one of my friends, Rachel, came up to me and asked me if I would like a leather coat.

Would I? I was speechless, but just for a moment. I told her that I had just prayed for one on Monday. She responded, "Oh, I wish I had given it to you earlier." She said someone had given it to her, and neither she nor her daughter wanted it. She hung it in her closet and every time she walked by it, she thought of me.

I was standing there in amazement of God's dazzling love for me. She brought it to me the next day and it was a perfect fit. I looked all over it for the tag that said, To Susan, With Love from Jesus. It was just overwhelming and brought tears to my eyes.

Since that day, I have experienced God's love and provision over and over and over again. I am still amazed every time God specifically answers one of my prayers, because it just proves what a personal and loving God He is, and He knows me.

I would love to challenge you: if you have never prayed specifically for your needs, begin to do so immediately. God loves to dazzle us with His blessings. It is important to remember, though, that we need to pray that His will be done and trust Him even when He does not answer the way you had hoped.

*Trust in the Lord with all your heart and lean not on your own understanding. In all your ways acknowledge Him and He will make your paths straight. Proverbs 3:5-6*

The key is to get to know God is always good and has your best in mind no matter what happens. Begin to trust His heart even when you can't trace His hand. This will enable you to trust and obey His plans for your life. Psalms 37:4 reinforces this truth:

*Delight yourself in the Lord and He will give you the desires of your heart.*

Now when things do not go as you had prayed, keep on trusting in the Lord that His ways are always best.

# THE PUNCHING BAG

2 Corinthians 4:6-10, 16-18 states:

*For God, who said, "Let light shine out of darkness, made his light shine in our hearts to give us the light of the knowledge of God's glory displayed in the face of Christ. But we have this treasure in jars of clay to show that this all-surpassing power is from God and not from us. We are hard pressed on every side, but not crushed; perplexed, but not in despair; persecuted, but not abandoned; struck down, but not destroyed. We always carry around in our body the death of Jesus, so that the life of Jesus may also be revealed in our body.*

*Therefore, we do not lose heart. Though outwardly we are wasting away, yet inwardly we are being renewed day by day. For our light and momentary troubles are achieving for us an eternal glory that far outweighs them all. So, we fix our eyes not on what is seen, but on what is unseen, since what is seen is temporary, but what is unseen is eternal.*

2 Corinthians 5:9-10 says,

*So, we make it our goal to please him, whether we are at home in the body or away from it. For we must all appear before the judgment seat of Christ, so that each of us may receive what is due us for the things done while in the body, whether good or bad.*

Today, as I was pondering my most recent emotional punch in the face, at first it was excruciating and painful and it wrecked my nerves. I surely didn't feel like I deserved it, but it came all the same. I had much anxiety over this yesterday, but after I followed God's response to this, I had calming peace and could see things more clearly. As I awoke this morning, and my husband and I had our devotional time together, God reminded me of how a punching bag works. Every time a punch is extended, it sends the bag reeling, but very soon, it pops up and regains its balance because of the weighted sand. It even continues to waver for a time, but soon, it will regain its upright position.

This is true for those of us who know Jesus and have made HIM to be our security. For me personally, I have had many blows that have left me reeling, such as verbal and emotional abuse, divorce, mental illness, rejection, financial challenges, the ups and downs with being a parent, seeing your children wander from Jesus, as well as all the challenges that come with being a single mom. Yet each hurdle made me run hard after Jesus. I can also testify that HE has never disappointed me or failed to calm and steady me in the storms of life. Francesca Battistelli sings a song entitled, 'CONSTANT' and that is exactly what God has proven to be in my life, my Constant.

So next time you are sent reeling by an emotional punch in the face, remember whose you are and who you belong to. Allow God to help you process the incident before you take action. Ask forgiveness if you are deserving of the punch, and if not, then focus on God's truth in the situation. Follow God's plan and remember that a 'soft answer turns away wrath' (Proverbs 15:1). You will soon regain the PEACE that only God can give in the storms of life.

I pray that God will bless you as you seek to make HIM your forever Constant and Security.

# COINCIDENCES OR DIVINE INTERVENTION?

A s I retold the story of how my husband Jay and I met, I knew I needed to write it down, so I would never forget the truth of listening to God's voice.

Maybe you remember how game shows would make you choose a number for a prize that was hidden. It might be a very nice prize, or it could be something very disappointing. You just had to make your guess and hope for the best, but choosing God's ways is not like this at all.

According to God's Word, His promises will never disappoint you, but there are steps of obedience we must take in order to receive His storehouse of blessings. Sometimes God's ways seem contrary to the way we are looking at things and they do not make sense. Sometimes God says, "No," to our immediate wishes, only so that He can give us something far greater than what we thought we wanted or needed. Ephesians 3:20-21 says it like this,

> *Now to Him who is able to do exceedingly abundantly above all that we ask or think, according to the power that works in us, to Him be glory in the church by Christ Jesus to all generations, forever and ever. Amen.*

This definitely requires trust in our Heavenly Father that He is good, and He is God. What I have learned is that trust is acquired when depending upon someone and they are constantly reliable to come through for me every single time. Experiencing God's amazing ways is how I have learned to trust and obey God even when I don't want to.

So, back to meeting Jay: I was working at the Health Department, and I was being forced into being the STD nurse, which I absolutely did not want, so I applied for another position in another clinic. Well, I was interviewed and offered the job, but in my heart, I knew that God did not want me to move, even though I felt desperate to escape the current situation. I knew I needed to obey God's leading, and I turned down the job offer.

A very short time later, I went to go get my next patient that needed a Hepatitis vaccination. When I inquired why he needed this, he told me that his doctor had recommended this to protect his liver, but his office had just run out of Hepatitis B vaccines, so he sent him to the Health Department to get it. We had a very nice conversation during that brief encounter, and I shared about the REACH Mentoring Ministry for foster youth, and he gave me his business card. There are more details to this story, but anyway, he called me six days later and asked me out.

We are now married and still dating, and I still can't believe how God has blessed us and turned both of our lives around.

I can't imagine how our lives would be different today had I not listened and obeyed the Lord's Spirit and accepted the other job in the other clinic. I would have utterly missed meeting my Prince Charming.

So, next time God asks you to trust His leading even when it goes against all that you desire, trust HIM, and watch God's amazing ways to unfold in your life.

# KOHL'S CASH

2 Corinthians 1:3-5 says,

*Praise be to the God and Father of our Lord Jesus Christ, the Father of compassion and the God of all comfort, who comforts us in all our troubles, so that we can comfort those in any trouble with the comfort we ourselves receive from God.*

Many years ago, when I was surviving yet thriving as a single mom, God used so many people in my life to demonstrate His love and provision for me and my sons, including my friend Maria. It was such a difficult time financially for me, so I was continually praying to God about my needs and sometimes even my wants. One of these times, I was needing new underwear and so I let God know about my need, since He cares about every detail of my life. Shortly after this prayer request was prayed privately, God led my friend to share with me the Kohl's Cash she had earned, though she had no idea about my need.

As she spoke with me, I just wanted to cry because I was continually experiencing God's lavish love and provision in my life. I had known God for many years before this, but this season of my life was absolutely unbelievable as I was so aware of how personally involved He was in my life with all the blessings that happened over and over and over again.

I love the verse in John 1:16 which says,

*Out of the fullness of His grace, we have received one blessing after another.*

This was truly my life. I used to say jokingly to others, "God loves you, but I'm His favorite." I never meant any disrespect, but I truly felt engulfed in His love and wanted everyone to know what a wonderful God we serve. He shows up in the darkness when we are most desperate for Him.

Obviously, I would never wish to repeat these painful years, but I can honestly say that I miss the intimacy with Jesus that I experienced during this season of my life.

Today, my friend is walking down a painful path as well, and as I was talking with her, I was able to share encouragement with her and remind her of how faithful God has been and will continue to be. I was able to bring comfort back to her as she has done so many times in my life.

Years ago, I compared my friends to some of my favorite flowers and Maria was my lilac. She was full of life and joy and just a sweet fragrance to me. So, today, I did not give her Kohl's Cash, but instead I bought her a lilac candle and hand soap to remind her that she is a fragrant offering to Jesus as she is allowing Him to direct her path step by step.

Whatever you may be going through today, trust Him to lead you and then allow Him to use you in others' lives to bring comfort to them as He has done for you.

# AT LEAST I'M NOT LIKE JONAH

Once, while flying to the Raleigh-Durham International Airport (RDU) from Ohio with a stop in Charlotte, North Carolina, I considered missing my connecting flight on purpose. It was my son Benjamin's birthday, and I would have loved to surprise him with a visit. This thought was planted in my mind when the airline announced that it had overbooked the flight, and they were offering cash to anyone willing to take a later flight. I didn't need the money necessarily like I have in the past, but the thought of seeing Benjamin was exciting to me.

When I got off the plane and headed to the gate for my connecting flight, I honestly was not sure that I would even make it to the B10 concourse in time. As I pondered this deviant and manipulative behavior and decision, I considered the implications and consequences since I was supposed to work the next day and had other responsibilities that would not be handled if I did not make it back in time.

Thankfully, I also considered what God would want me to do, for ultimately, I truly desire to please the Lord with all my actions and decisions. I realized too that all our choices and decisions have a domino effect. Everything I do in some way affects others around us either positively or negatively.

I made it to the concourse in time and proceeded to do the right thing by boarding the plane to RDU to go home. As I sat on the plane waiting to take off, I pondered and evaluated how God has a plan for each of us as well as assignments and ministry each day. If we fail to show up, be present and accounted for, we have no idea how that can impact someone else's life and future. This reminded me of Jonah who ran from God's plans for his life (Jonah 1). He had a different idea of what he wanted to do, rather than follow through with God's plan and purpose for him at the specific time.

Through my years of learning from the Bible, I have likely judged Jonah and frowned in disapproval, yet I realized that I have probably done this over and over in my life.

*Judge not, that ye be not judged. Matthew 7:1*

Way too often, I have weighed the pros and cons of God's directives instead of just walking in obedience, especially prior to doing the Experiencing God Bible Study. I had usually asked God to bless my plans rather than seek His plans for me.

Not only did Jonah face hardship because of his choice to resist God, but others' lives and livelihoods were greatly impacted in a detrimental way.

Heavenly Father, please forgive me for so often going my own way and often causing lack or hardship to others because I failed to show up for Your assignments for the day. Please help me to stop and listen to Your voice and Your Holy Spirit's instructions and really learn this vital lesson from Jonah's life. Please help me to walk in obedience to You in every choice and decision I make. In Jesus' name, Amen.

# SAD? GO AND BLESS SOMEONE!

I am thankful I remembered something my mom had told me a long time ago. She said, "When you feel down and discouraged, go find someone to bless and encourage them and it will lift your own spirits as well as the other person." Well, I was very discouraged at the time. I was in nursing school and overwhelmed with my classes but also my life in general. I was a single mom taking care of my two sons. I wanted to give in and feel sorry for myself, but I decided to practice my mom's advice and Ms. Priest came to my mind.

Now, Ms. Priest was a dear lady whom I had recently met at Smithfield Manor Nursing Home. She had been one of my patients during my nursing clinical rotation and she was a pure delight. She had been blind for many years and lived on her own, but she had suffered a stroke and so she had to move out of her home and into the nursing home. She had an amazing smile and laugh and never once complained about her current health concerns and situation. She actually asked how I was doing, and it was amazing to see her countenance radiate with God's love, joy, and peace. She was also quick to let me know that she personally knew Jesus and had walked with him many years.

As I considered what might bless her, I was mindful that though she could not see, she could still hear, smell, taste and feel. So, I mixed up a batch of chocolate chip cookies, which I figured was everyone's favorite cookie, wrote her a note with some Scriptures on it and then proceeded to purchase a hyacinth flower, which smells absolutely amazing to me.

I went to Walmart, but they were sold out of those flowers. I then went to Lowes and asked an employee if they had any hyacinths left. I explained the situation and let her know that I really needed them. She let me know that there might be some ready to be thrown out because they were old and wilting. She led me to them, and she helped me gather a bouquet. I told her they did not have to be perfect because my friend was blind. They smelled amazing, and I knew that when she felt them, she would not notice or care that they might be wilted.

When I showed up for my visit with her, her response was just as I had expected—completely grateful for me taking the time to bless her, baking yummy cookies, and bringing her the bouquet of flowers (I never told her they were wilted). She totally blessed me and lifted my spirits. Doing for someone else made me take my focus off myself and my problems and shift it onto someone else. My mom was so wise in sharing this truth with me and it works!

*Give, and it will be given to you. A good measure, pressed down, shaken together, and running over, will be poured into your lap. Luke 6:38*

# BUCKETS VS. CONDUITS

Not too long ago, I had been going through quite a bit of opposition in my workplace, and none of it really made sense in the natural realm. My friend, Angeline, shared with me that if things don't make sense in the natural world, you probably have supernatural warfare going on. I believe this to be true so I was striving to press into Jesus so I could become more like HIM through this and other difficult situations.

As I was spending time with Jesus, I was reminded of my favorite word—CONDUIT. For many years, this has been my word because it is such a visual representation of what I believe God desires our lives to be like. He wants us to allow His love to flow in us and then out through us to the people around us.

*All men/women will know that we are His disciples by our love for one another. John 13:35*

This is the desire of my heart, but way too often, I am more like an empty and dry bucket waiting to be filled by others. Then I am sadly disappointed when others fail to meet my needs that really only Jesus can supply.

I had also been reading a book about living like we are in the Kingdom of Heaven, and how there is no slander, gossip, backbiting or evil speaking about others in the Kingdom. We are to be representatives of the Kingdom and so often I realize I fall short.

While I was meditating, God led me to read Hebrews 12:1-14:

*Therefore, since we are surrounded by such a great cloud of witnesses, let us throw off everything that hinders and the sin that so easily entangles. And let us run with perseverance the race marked out for us, fixing our eyes on Jesus, the pioneer and perfecter of faith. For the joy set before him he endured the cross, despised the shame, and sat down at the right hand of the throne of God. Consider him who endured such opposition from sinners, so that you will not grow weary and lose heart.*

*In your struggle against sin, you have not yet resisted to the point of shedding your blood. And have you completely forgotten this word of encouragement that addresses you as a father addresses his son? It says, "My son, do not make light of the Lord's discipline, and do not lose heart when he rebukes you, because the Lord disciplines the one he loves, and he chastens everyone he accepts as his son. Endure hardship as discipline; God is treating you as his children. For what children are not disciplined by their father? If you are not disciplined—and everyone undergoes discipline—then you are not legitimate, not true sons and daughters at all. Moreover, we have all had human fathers who disciplined us and we respected them for it. How much more should we submit to the Father of spirits and live! They disciplined us for a little while as they thought best; but God disciplines us for our good, in order that we may share in his holiness. No discipline seems pleasant at the time, but painful. Later on, however, it produces a harvest of righteousness and peace for those who have been trained by it.*

*Therefore, strengthen your feeble arms and weak knees. "Make level paths for your feet, so that the lame may not be disabled, but rather healed.*

*Make every effort to live in peace with everyone and to be holy; without holiness no one will see the Lord.*

I especially love verse 14b, and it continues to be in my thoughts. WITHOUT HOLINESS, NO ONE WILL SEE THE LORD. This should be the goal of all of our lives that others will see Jesus in us. When we encounter trouble, we have a choice to let our light shine or react according to how we are being treated. Sadly, we often give in to our fleshly desires, but God promises to help us in our days of trouble. All we have to do is call on Jesus to help us obey His ways and His will moment by moment. In the end, when we obey, we will display the joy of the Lord in spite of all our challenges and trials.

Let's choose JOY and OBEDIENCE and ask God to give us a willing heart to live according to His Word. I'm in! I hope you will join me too.

# ASK AND YOU SHALL RECEIVE

I was sharing with a friend about how God led me to my first job at Johnston Memorial Hospital and then later that same day, I ran into Donna, who hired me. As I reflected on God's faithfulness to answer my prayers, I decided to share how another one of God's promises came true in my life.

*If you, then, though you are evil, know how to give good gifts to your children, how much more will your Father in heaven give good gifts to those who ask him! Matthew 7:11*

I have experienced that God is the best ever gift Giver!

Back in 2007, I was stressed to the max trying to finish up nursing school, while many of my classmates were consumed with trying to land their first job as a nurse. Observing them, honestly, stressed me out more, because I had no idea which area of nursing would be best for me. One day after classes, I took a walk around the pond at Johnston Community College and prayed, first, that I would graduate, and secondly, that God would provide a job for me. I prayed specifically that since I was not sure where I needed to work, someone would just offer me a job so I would not have to worry about where to apply.

Well, later that week, I went to the hospital for my clinical rotation and my supervisor, Donna, called me into her office. She reminded me that she had already said she would like me to work for her when I graduated and that her offer was still available if I would like to work there. I told her I would definitely like to accept her offer as I believed that this was the direct answer to prayer that I had just recently prayed.

I was inwardly rejoicing at how much God loves me, hears my prayers, knows me by name, knows exactly where I need to be and what is best for me in every area of my life. The old hymn, Tis So Sweet to Trust in Jesus, says it best:

> *'Tis so sweet to trust in Jesus, just to take Him at His Word, just to rest upon His promise,*
> *Jesus, Jesus, how I trust Him! How I've proved Him o'er and o'er.*

Oh, how I love this verse because God has proved Himself faithful to me over and over and over. I need His grace to trust Him more each time a new challenge comes my way so I can faithfully finish the race that God has given me to run, and one day Jesus will say, "Well done, Susan." I pray that you too will be able to say with me that Jesus has been proven faithful over and over.

# LOVING ONE ANOTHER

I have often heard that when children leave the home, it keeps you on your knees more than when they are little. I have lived out some painful seasons, but I have also been blessed above anything I could ever have imagined.

My sons have been very different, but they have always had a strong love for each other. However, back in 2017, my sons had a serious breach of relationship, and my heart was so broken.

*An offended brother is more unyielding than a fortified city, and disputes are like the barred gates of a citadel. Proverbs 18:19a*

This was very true in our lives at this time, and it was so hard as a mom to see my children making choices as adults that could have serious and permanent repercussions and not be able to do anything to change it.

It was during the time when my youngest son was preparing for his wedding. He and his brother were very divided over a very tough and sensitive issue, and they just did not see eye to eye. This resulted in a very painful time for everyone involved. I wanted to fix things and mend them up, but there was just nothing I could do except pray. I had talked until there was nothing more to say. I was so happy that God had provided a wonderful wife for my son, but the other part of my heart was completely torn apart over the loss of relationship between my sons. I made it through the day with many tears. Thankfully people just thought they were emotional happy tears, and so I did not have to discuss why I was crying.

Fast forward to a couple years later and God has miraculously worked in my son's lives. They are reunited to a certain point. God is still working on each of them and helping them to navigate some very difficult situations and loving each other through the differences. Through it all, God is teaching me so much and giving me grace to love no matter where a person is in their life.

*Above all, love each other deeply, because love covers over a multitude of sins. I Peter 4:8*

*By this all men will know that you are my disciples, if you love one another. John 13:35*

So, wherever you may find yourself today, don't give up. Remember to keep on praying for your children because God is a God who loves to restore broken things and people. His extravagant love is what draws us to repentance, so let's become conduits of His love to allow His love to draw our children to Himself.

# YOU CAN'T PLAY HIDE AND SEEK WITH JESUS!

Psalms 139:1-4 states:

*O Lord, you have searched me and you know me. You know when I sit and when I rise, you perceive my thoughts from afar. You discern my going out and my lying down; you are familiar with all my ways. Before a word is on my tongue you know it completely, O Lord. Vs. 7 – 12, Where can I go from your Spirit? Where can I flee from your presence? If I go up to the heavens, you are there if I make my bed in the depths, you are there. If I rise on the wings of the dawn, if I settle on the far side of the sea, even there your hand will guide me, your right hand will hold me fast. If I say, "Surely the darkness will hide me, and the light becomes night around me, even the darkness will not be dark to you; the night will shine like the day for darkness is as light to you."*

Earlier this year, God answered one of my prayers, AMAZINGLY and made me realize that we can never play hide and seek with God. Here's what happened: In 2020, I was using a small, red prayer journal to record my prayer requests. Sometime in September of 2020, I misplaced this journal and could not find it. I always kept it in my tote bag with my Bible, so I knew I probably lost it at church. I have learned from previous life experiences that God is able to reveal where things are hidden, so I had prayed about finding this journal many times. However, after months and months of it missing, I knew there was a good possibility that I would not find it. Still, I was confident that God knew exactly where it was.

Well, on June 8, 2021, I was at First Baptist Church preparing for the REACH summer camp we were doing for four foster girls. As

I was speaking to Margie in the office, and she told me she wanted to show me something. She went back to her office and brought out a little red prayer journal and asked me if this belonged to me. I could not believe my eyes. It was mine! She told me it did not even have my name on it, but flipping through some of the pages, she saw the name Stem and thought of me. God just blows my mind sometimes.

He is ever so faithful to delight us and answer our simple prayers. As I pondered the goodness of God and that He knows where everything is hidden under the ground, in the oceans, in our pockets, or at the bottom of our purses or tote bags, I realized that it is not wise to try to play hide and seek games with God. He will always win! Just as in the garden of Eden, when Adam and Eve tried to hide, God pursued them and lovingly questioned them. He already knew, but He gave them an opportunity to confess and be restored into fellowship with Him.

Anyone who knows me knows that I love to play games. I pray, though, that I will learn to never try to hide from Jesus because of my sinful actions, but to run into His open arms and be restored into fellowship with the best and dearest Friend, Father, and the Lover of my soul.

# WORRY OR PRAY

Another year has rolled around; we have entered 2021, and closed out 2020, praise God! We experienced a pandemic that sent the world into chaos, confusion, hopelessness, financial struggles, job loss, and the biggest of all, FEAR! Everyone had to deal with unexpected issues this year and I was not an exception to this.

Now, I have learned so many lessons over my years of walking with the Lord and one major truth He has taught me is that I can truly trust and depend on the Lord. However, in order to apply this belief, I must demonstrate my faith by obeying what He tells me to do. The second part is the hardest.

I have been drawn into sweet fellowship with the Lord during the most intense times of trials, and I felt like I was actually in an incubator with Jesus. The fire was raging all around me, but I did not feel it, nor was I permanently harmed by it. God used the fire to burn up many ropes of sin that were in my heart just like Shadrach, Meshach, and Abednego when they were thrown into the fiery furnace. Their clothes did not smell of smoke, nor was their hair singed, nor were they harmed in any way. King Nebuchadnezzar even saw a fourth man in the fire with them, who was the Son of God.

During this past year, I have witnessed the paralyzing fear of getting COVID 19. I realized that the root of the fear is dying. I have said many times that most importantly, we should be evaluating WHERE we will go when we die, instead of HOW we will die. We all have an expiration date on our lives that God alone knows, and we can trust HIM to take care of us until He calls us home.

So, although I have not struggled with the fear of dying, I realized that I was still afraid in areas I needed to surrender to Jesus and cast my cares upon Him. Specifically, how our world is upside down and what God says is sin, our world celebrates. Seeing the promotion of the New World Order or the Great Reset. What God says is honorable, the world disdains and throws away. As I am aware what the Bible states will happen in the last days before Jesus comes back, the fear of persecution and suffering was rising up in me. My dear husband, Jay, has reminded me more than once, that I can either worry or pray, but I cannot do both, but too often I have wrestled with trying not to worry. I am so thankful that God keeps lovingly reminding me of His past faithfulness to me and that I can trust Him again today and every day for the rest of my life.

Father, help me to trust you and listen and obey Your voice no matter what happens in my lifetime for I am convinced this is the key to the Christian life. Philippians 4:6 says it best:

*Do not worry or be anxious about anything, but in every situation, by prayer and petition, with thanksgiving, present your requests to God.*

# GET DRESSED BEFORE YOU GO OUT

I was reminded of a very embarrassing time while I was serving as a houseparent for the Christian Life Home. I had gone out early one morning to have my devotions on the back porch, and when I had finished, I realized I had locked myself out. I panicked since I had not put on a robe over my gown. I ran to the front door, but it was locked. I tried the window, but it, too, was locked. I remembered that I had opened the side window earlier that week, but it was very high above the ground. I went back around the house to the storage building, found a ladder and proceeded to carry it to the window. I climbed up, discovered the window was still unlocked and managed to hoist myself safely inside. Boy, was I relieved!

As I was rehearsing this event in my mind, and laughing to myself, it reminded me of the importance of God's words to us from Ephesians 6:10-18.

*Finally, be strong in the Lord and in His mighty power. Put on the full armor of God, so that you can take your stand against the devil's schemes. For our struggle is not against flesh and blood, but against the rulers, against the authorities, against the powers of this dark world and against the spiritual forces of evil in the heavenly realms. Therefore, put on the full armor of God, so that when the day of evil comes, you may be able to stand your ground, and after you have done everything, to stand. Stand firm then, with the belt of truth buckled around your waist, with the breastplate of righteousness in place, and with your feet fitted with the readiness that comes from the gospel of peace. In addition to all this, take up the shield of faith, with which you can extinguish all the flaming arrows of the evil one. Take the helmet of salvation and the sword of the Spirit, which is the word of God. Pray in the Spirit on all occasions with all kinds of prayers and requests. With this in mind, be alert and always keep on praying for all the Lord's people.*

As I review my life, so many times I have failed to prepare myself for the enemy's attacks and have suffered many painful consequences as a result. What can be even worse is when your choices affect those around you. The Bible says in John 10:10:

*Satan comes to steal, kill and destroy, but Jesus came so that we may have an abundant life.*

God instructs us how to stand strong against the enemy and be victorious.

So, remember to get dressed physically and spiritually before you go out and trust and obey God's instructions for an abundant life!

# GRASSHOPPERS IN OUR OWN EYES

Numbers 13 records the time when Moses sent twelve spies to the land God had promised to the Israelites. Ten of them came back with a bad report that there were giants in the land, and that they were like grasshoppers in their own eyes. Only Joshua and Caleb came back trusting God's promises and believed that they would be victorious in conquering this new land. The Israelites listened to the bad report and as a result, they wandered for the wilderness for forty years until they all died. They never made it to the Promised Land. The ten spies made a decision based on their own thoughts and insecurities instead of trusting God's promises. I have often done this as well.

I was reminded of a day when I was in third grade. I loved my teacher, Ms. Hawes and always felt I was one of her favorites. I did well in school and loved getting her positive comments on my papers. I wanted her to be proud of me.

Well, one cold day, I wore a hat to school, but it was really to cover up my new pixie haircut, which I despised. My teacher requested I remove the hat and put it in my locker. I reluctantly did as she asked and returned to the classroom with major static in my hair. I was so embarrassed and felt like everyone was staring at me. I sat down in my seat and just wanted to disappear.

Well, many years later, during a counseling session, this humiliating memory popped up in my mind. My counselor prompted me to ask Jesus where He was during that time. I asked and waited but did not sense an answer. My counselor proceeded to ask me questions, such as, did anyone laugh or make fun of me? I responded that I didn't remember anyone even mentioning it. As I continued to ask Him where He was that time, I chuckled because I thought he must have blinded their eyes. God's protection must have made them oblivious because I did not recall one comment or derogatory remark. I realize now that my humiliation was due to the lies Satan put into my own head about how ugly my hair was.

What a liar Satan is, and I now realize that his tactics are the same as he has always used. He lies to us about the goodness of God and causes us to doubt God and believe God is holding out on us. Satan lies to us that we are ugly, not important, not valuable, and unloved. Then life's circumstances reinforce the lies over and over and over again until they become a powerful stronghold. These strongholds can become more powerful than God's promises and can keep us from entering our Promised Land. God has a plan(s) and a purpose(s) for our lives, but Satan comes to steal, kill, and destroy all that God has promised.

So today, are you believing you *can do all things through Christ and that we are more than conquerors through Him who strengthens us?* (Philippians 4:13, Romans 8:31) Or, are you seeing yourself as a grasshopper?

> *Take every thought captive and make them obedient to Christ. 2 Corinthians 10:5b*

Trust what God's words say about who you are and what you can do through Him!

# GREEN MINT CHOCOLATE CHIP ICE CREAM

What a happy birthday party we had on January 21, 2003. It did not look very promising in the beginning planning stages, BUT GOD. When God steps into something, He changes everything down to the smallest detail, just to bless our socks off!

It was my youngest son, John-Mark's tenth birthday and I wanted to honor him. I was praying about God's provision for this event because I was without an income at the time. I asked John-Mark what his wishes were, and he said, "Kentucky Fried Chicken, BBQ chips and green mint chocolate chip ice cream." He has always loved the color green. Well, I am not sure how many of you have tried to locate green mint chocolate chip ice cream, but it is not as easy to find compared to white mint chocolate chip ice cream. Anyway, John-Mark shared his wishes, and I began planning.

I had not mentioned our needs to anyone, but I soon received a call from our dear friend, Donna, and she offered to help me plan the party. She offered to bring Kentucky Fried Chicken, plates, and BBQ chips. Just a little while later, another dear friend, also named Donna, called and asked how she could help. I mentioned the green mint chocolate chip ice cream, which might be difficult to locate. Her response blew me away. She said, "I just bought a gallon of that the day before and I'm not sure why, because my family does not even like it." I knew that God was already preparing to give John-Mark the desire of his heart and lavishly showing His love and favor in his life.

*Delight yourself in the Lord and He will give you the desires of your heart. Psalms 37:4*

I had homeschooled both my sons, and after John-Mark learned to read, he read his Bible faithfully every morning as soon as he woke up and strived to honor the Lord in everything He did. It brought such joy to my heart to catch him sitting in his bed in the morning reading. It was honestly amazing to watch him grow up with such a strong desire to place God first in his life and he received back honor from others and the Lord.

I'm so thankful to have witnessed God's blessing in giving him the desires of his heart, even down to the exact type of ice cream he requested.

God has allowed some very harsh storms to come into our family, but through even the darkest of times, God continued to dazzle us with His lavish provision even down to the smallest of details. Through this, God enabled us to know He was our Provider.

*Your Father knows what you need before you ask Him. Matthew 6:8b*

I am so thankful for the lessons He has taught us and for the confidence we can have in Jesus Christ that *He will supply all of our needs when we place Him first in our lives* (Matthew 6:33, Philippians 4:19).

# WHOSE HAND IS THE PAINTBRUSH IN?

One of the most fun and adventurous people I have ever known was Georgie Brothers. Once, while visiting her, she told me about a hilarious prank she pulled while she was vacationing in France viewing the sights. She said she walked up to an artist painting on a canvas. She tried to communicate with him unsuccessfully since they spoke different languages. Finally, she was able to convey through gestures she wanted to hold his paintbrush and he gave it to her very reluctantly. She proceeded to sit down and lifted the paintbrush up to the canvas as if to continue to paint. She said the man became frantic, frightened she might touch the canvas. She ignored him and had her photo taken by her friend and finally handed the brush back to the man.

This reminded me of how often we snatch the paintbrush out of our Master's hands when we don't like all the strokes and harsh colors He allows to be blended into our lives. We quickly doubt His love and care for us. We focus on the incomplete picture and forget the Master Designer has plans for a beautiful portrait of our lives.

BUT, when we rip the paintbrush out of His hand, we can make a huge mess of our lives. We think we know best and refuse to trust God.

> *ALL things work together for good for those who love God and are called according to His purpose. Romans 8:28*

This does not say that ALL things *are* good, but that ALL things *work for our* good which is a huge difference. One thing I have learned is this: the more time we spend with Jesus, the more we get to know Him, which leads us to trust Him and His ways.

So, the next time you are ready to take a situation into your own hands and paint your own picture, think about this. Let's learn from the words of Solomon, the wisest man ever on the earth:

*Trust in the Lord with all your heart, and lean not on your own understanding. In all your ways acknowledge Him, and He will make your paths straight. Proverbs 3:5-6*

# STUCK BETWEEN THE EGYPTIANS AND THE RED SEA

Have you ever heard the quote, stuck between a rock and a hard place? Well, Moses and all the Israelites knew what that was like when they left Egypt through God's miraculous deliverance. They probably thought, finally we are free. Just as they were breathing a sigh of relief and were nearing the Red Sea, they realized that the Egyptians were in hot pursuit of them. They looked to Moses for help, and God directed him to guide them straight into the sea! Yikes! But as they walked forward, God parted the water, and they were saved at the last minute.

If you have walked with Jesus for any amount of time at all, you have probably learned that God is never early, but He is always on time. These are the times that stretch our faith and teach us to trust that God is good and faithful, and He WILL provide for His children.

My son Benjamin found himself in a situation like this in 2013. He was accepted into the Respiratory Therapy Program at Carteret Community College where there are no dormitories, so we were diligently looking for living arrangements, with no success. In addition, we were informed there were no more student loans for community colleges which we had anticipated to assist us. We felt backed up against a wall, and as a single mom, I did not have the financial resources to assist him.

We were definitely praying just like Jehoshaphat did when an army was preparing to attack Israel:

*O our God, we have no power to face this vast army that is attacking us. We do not know what to do, but our eyes are upon you.* 2 Chronicles 20:12

Well, just like God did with the Israelites, He came through for us in just the nick of time. We had been praying and investigating every possibility. I had reached out to a pastor friend there and he directed me to the director of the Atlantic Baptist Association. After meeting David and sharing our dilemma, he and his wife willingly offered to open their home for Benjamin to live there for a couple of weeks, until he could locate a more permanent place. Benjamin accepted this generous offer and was immediately welcomed into their family with love and support. We also were introduced to another local pastor in Morehead, who was a cousin to my friend, Angie. Jerry and his wife agreed to allow Benjamin to rent a room from them for the next two years. He was treated more as a son than a tenant and was loved, prayed for, and supported. Benjamin experienced such wonderful examples of a godly marriage and relationship with these two families that he would have never experienced if we would not have been in such a hard place.

Looking back at the way God provided for Benjamin during that season of His life, I can only praise Him for showing Himself mighty on our behalf. I know how difficult it was for us to learn to trust God, but I can testify that, as a result, we KNOW and are confident that if God can do it for us then, He can do it again. Praise God from whom all blessings flow! Do it again, Lord!

# SENIOR LIVING FOR OUR PETS

While raising my sons as a single parent, we had a cat named Sassy, a beagle named Shiloh and a golden retriever, Hunny.

Shiloh was John-Mark's dog. She was a beagle that loved to track in the woods. Her sister, Duchess, had been Benjamin's dog, but due to a leg injury that did not heal from tracking in the woods, she had to be put down. Duchess had been at the top of the pecking order, so now Shiloh had an opportunity to have all the attention.

Well, at this time in John-Mark's life, he was gone a lot on the weekends and school was taking up more of his time. He just did not have much time to devote to loving and caring for Shiloh. We all felt bad about not giving her the attention she deserved.

John-Mark and I discussed this and then we prayed together that we would find a loving retirement home for Shiloh. It was not long after this that John-Mark came home from his CrossWave Youth Group and told me about his friend, Carlos who had mentioned that he and his wife were looking for a female, older beagle that could be kept indoors. This description matched Shiloh one hundred percent. We contacted them and they came over to meet Shiloh and immediately fell in love with her. Shortly after this initial meeting when John-Mark had time to say his goodbyes, we arranged to have her relocate and live with Carlos and Christina. They did not have any children yet, so they completely doted on Shiloh, let her sleep in the bed with them and she became their baby. Shiloh lived for several years after this move and I am sure she was blessed so much in her little doggy heart.

his story reminds me of how God loves us enough to even consider our requests for our pets and gives them more than they could have even barked for.

As a sequel and parallel situation, our cat Sassy also relocated to a loving home. She had always been an outdoor cat who was faithful to stick around our home, until we got our dog Hunny, who liked to chase her. Sassy began spending more and more time at our neighbor's house. They began feeding her and we saw her less and less. Finally, our neighbor's mom was looking for a cat and had already established a relationship with Sassy while visiting her daughter, Gwen. Ms. Jean eventually asked me if she could have Sassy come live with her. Because I realized Sassy was not comfortable any longer in our home, I was happy to let Sassy move. Ms. Jean provided her with lots of love, treats and a cozy little cat house in her heated garage. One of the last times I visited Sassy, she was as round as a butterball and seemed as happy as she could be.

I am so thankful Jesus hears our prayers and works on our behalf to lovingly care for our pets. Father God, You, are such an awesome Provider.

*A righteous man cares for the needs of his animals. Proverbs 12:10*

# BE IT UNTO ME

One morning I decided to take a walk before I went to work. I walked around the Johnston Community College lake as I had done many times before and I began praying for my family and some hard situations I was dealing with. I acknowledged that He was using these situations to create in me a heart that looks more like HIM.

I prayed what Mary, the mother of Jesus, prayed in Luke 1:38:

*I am Your servant, be it unto me according to Your word.*

It was then an angel approached her with the amazing news that she would give birth to Jesus. She immediately made a decision to accept God's plan for her life in spite of all that she would have to face as a result of her pregnancy. It didn't appear that she stopped to consider the possible painful situations she might have to endure, such as rejection by her fiancé, gossiping in the community and possibly even death by stoning. Instead, she recognized that it was an angel of God, and she received the message with joy. It reminded me that God sends people and situations into our lives for a purpose.

I thanked God for reminding me that just because situations are hard, it does not mean that God is not working. As I was walking, I saw an old friend, Stephanie, who was headed to her next class. We caught up with each other and she asked me about my son, Benjamin, who she had previously taught at Johnston Community College, and said she had a special love and appreciation for him. Then she changed the topic of our children to what she just recently studied in her Bible study about Mary, the mother of Jesus. She shared how the conception of Jesus could have led to rejection, but she had God's favor on her life because Jesus was with her and now in her. Mary's response was, "Be it unto me as You have desired/requested/required."

I almost began crying as I shared with her that I had just been praying the very same words she just spoke. God was so sweet to confirm this truth, reminding us that we are His daughters, and He is very involved in our lives in every situation, and He desires us to rest in His care and not question Him.

*Yet you, LORD, are our Father. We are the clay; you are the potter; we are all the work of your hand. Isaiah 64:8*

*But who are you, a human being, to talk back to God? Shall what is formed say to the one who formed it, 'Why did you make me like this?' Romans 9:20*

Jesus, help me to remember I am Your highly favored servant, You are with me and in me, just like Mary. Help me to trust Your process and accept with joy all that You have sent my way. I know You are God and You have been so good to me. Help me to forgive and bear with other's issues that affect my life. Help me to strive to see them through Your eyes of love.

Oh Father, thank you for seeing me and speaking clearly to me this day through Your Holy Spirit and my friend, Stephanie. I had prayed to hear Your voice and for You to fill me with Yourself and it was pure joy to have You respond so quickly to my request. You are an awesome and amazing God.

# BLACK AND WHITE NOTES

I was given a keyboard from my sweet mother-in-love, Edna, one Christmas. I had always wanted to learn how to play the piano and even took lessons a couple of times at Johnston Community College. As I was plinking out the notes for some easy songs, I was learning about the chords and the black notes. I had never pondered why there are both black and white notes on the keyboard, but they definitely sound different. The white keys are more harmonious, and the black keys are discordant and often sound like fingernails on a chalkboard if they are not played as they were intended to be.

As I thought about this, I realized my life has had both white and black keys playing. Some of my life has been blessed and harmonious but I have also experienced some very painful trials. However, I can look back over my life and see how God has used all of the experiences and situations in my life to make my life more beautiful and to help conform me to look more like HIM. I can see His fingerprints all over my life, now in retrospect.

Here's a few examples: I was not in the popular crowd and was excluded from being invited to parties while I was in elementary school, but God was actually protecting me from some of the situations that happened during them. My church had a split and the Christian school I attended almost closed since so many teachers left, but God led me to a different Christian school where I was able to graduate early with important classes which prepared me for two jobs that I got later in life. I married my college sweetheart only to be divorced seventeen years later, but God has restored my life with a wonderful marriage to Jay Stem. I became a single mom with no job or income, but God led me to go back to school for nursing. I was no longer able to homeschool my sons, but God provided a dear family that paid for two years of Christian school for my sons. I became a needy single mom, but God opened up the Heavens and poured out blessings and provisions on our lives. My house was robbed, but God directed me to a program that provided scholarships to help me go through nursing school and even provided gas money. I began cleaning houses and when I would lose one house, God gave me a new one located closer to my son's school and my college. I had the rug pulled out from under me becoming a single parent, but God actually drew me closer to Him than ever before and I realized what an awesome Father, Friend, Provider and Sustainer He really is. My desire was fulfilled when both of my sons attended Word of Life Bible College, but God allowed them to go through severe emotional and health challenges during and afterwards. I love my sons, yet we have gone through hard challenges during their adulthood, but God keeps teaching me what loving like Jesus really should look like.

I could truly go on and on about how blessings and hardships all work together for our good and God's glory, just like the keys on a piano. When played by the pianist, it is a melodious sound, delightful to our ears. I am so thankful we serve a *God who causes all things to work together for the good of those that love Him and are called according to His purpose* (Romans 8:28).

# ONE AMAZING FAMILY

It was not that many years ago that I was a single mom, studying for a nursing degree at Johnston Community College. I remember very well all of the challenges I faced to provide financially for my sons by cleaning houses, and the grueling hours required to study. I know that God alone carried me during those years and thankfully, He sent many others to help lift the load for me. One of the many angels was the Hodgins family.

I met them at Colonial Baptist Church where I attended a single-parenting class. They had a huge heart for single parents and wanted to help in any way they could. They made numerous visits to my home to help me with projects around the house. They selflessly served with great sacrifices by driving over an hour to my house with their four children and ministered together. Over and over, they poured into our lives.

It was during this time that I was trying to secure a lawyer and the retainer fee was $2500. I had no idea how this need would be met but I was praying and doing all I could to work and save. It was one of the days that their family came to my house and as they were leaving for the day, they handed me $2,500. They stated that God had blessed them, and they knew that they needed to give this to me. I was absolutely speechless at their amazing generosity.

Dale had actually quit his job in technology and was starting a new company with the sole purpose of training single parents in computer skills to help them survive and thrive.

2 Corinthians 8:3 says,

> *For I testify that they gave as much as they were able, and even beyond their ability.*

Dale and Chris had such huge hearts, and I am convinced their hearts were even bigger than their pocketbooks, since their company was just getting started.

I am also very thankful for Dale's excellent computer skills, his willingness to take my calls and help me become more proficient with the computer while I was in nursing school. He had great patience with me during my learning curves and helped me with remote access to my computer.

During one of these sessions, he realized that I needed a new computer for my nursing classes. One morning, I received a call from Dale, and he asked me where I was. I had just arrived in the Johnston Community College parking lot. They said they needed to stop by and see me. In a couple of minutes, they pulled up, got out of their car, and handed me a case with a brand-new computer inside. Again, I was speechless at their amazing generosity.

I still can't believe how God took care of all of my needs through the wonderful people that He placed in my life during this time. They continue to be amazing conduits of His love for me and so many others and I will never forget all the ways they lovingly ministered to my family. I will always thank Jesus for putting them in our lives.

# OH, JAKE

Jake was a good, gentle dog who had been such a wonderful companion to Jay during some of his hardest days. If you ask Jay, he will even attribute his very life to Jake. So, I will always be grateful for Jake.

Jake survived a stroke and struggled with some health issues, primarily bowel incontinence. He could not help this, but it was hard for me to deal with. Jay used our carpet shampooer more often than I care to mention. I would think to myself, "Oh, Jake."

Today, as I was having my quiet time with Jesus, I pondered my frustration with Jake's issues. I was pricked in my heart when I wondered how often my Heavenly Father might say, "Oh, Susan." I know He loves me lavishly and I never truly want to offend Him, yet I mess up again and again. My goal is to please Jesus with my life, but my sin is much like Jake's poop: it stinks, it's unsanitary, it defiles me and others and someone has to clean it up. I might walk around in it or try to hide it, and I may even return to it again and again. When I am caught, I might just act like nothing is a problem and respond with that, "What?" look on my face.

So often we live our lives without any regard for the holy standards of our Lord. Can you imagine what a stench our sin is to Jesus? Isaiah 64:6-7 describes *our righteous acts as filthy rags to God*. So, imagine what a stench our sin is to Him, if even our righteousness doesn't even measure up to His holiness? Jesus was willing to take all of our sins upon Him and be crucified on the cross so that He could provide a way for us to go to heaven and have fellowship for all eternity with our Creator.

Isaiah 53:4-6 states,

> *Surely, he took our pain and bore our suffering… He was pierced for our transgressions, He was crushed for our iniquities; the punishment that brought us peace was on him, and by his wounds we are healed. We have all gone astray and turned to our own way; and the Lord has laid on Him the sins of us all.*

God sent Jesus to bring us peace and healing and fellowship with Him. I am so thankful God was willing to forgive us. Isaiah 1:18 says,

> *Come now, let us settle the matter," says the LORD. "Though your sins are like scarlet, they shall be as white as snow.*

Jake has gone to be with Jesus so I do not have to clean up after him any longer, but I hope that I will remember these truths. I will continue to strive for holiness, so that I will achieve my goal of pleasing Jesus. I hope this will be your goal as well, so that one day, Jesus will say, *Well done, thou good and faithful servant. Enter into my rest* (Matthew 25:23).

# TUMBLING TOWERS

Have you ever played the game Jenga? Well, if you have not, it consists of stacking up blocks of wood and then each person takes turns removing one piece with the goal of not having it fall.

I recently encountered a situation which reminded me of this game. I felt God wanted me to tell a person that had hurt me very badly that I had forgiven them. Now, in my heart I had tried to do this already, but I had never told the person. This was definitely a test of obedience God was offering me. I really did not want to do this, but God would not quit messing with me until finally around 11 pm, I texted them, "I forgive you." Short and sweet.

I followed through with obedience and I realized that often when God requests something of us, we may not understand the reason why. However, we need to trust and obey God's promptings.

Just like the Jenga game, as one wooden block removed can tumble the tower, so our words have the power to soften hardened hearts and bring healing. This, in turn, can be replicated in other people's lives when we take the first step towards reconciliation.

King Solomon, wisest king ever, wrote in Proverbs 18:21a:

*The tongue has the power of life and death.*

This is also God's will for everyone according to Romans 12:18:

*If it is possible, as far as it depends on you, live at peace with everyone.*

Because I desire to please the Lord, I strive to choose to speak life words.

When we obey God's instructions, we have confidence before the Lord, and we can pray that God uses our words and actions to bring life and soften hearts. I pray that my words will demonstrate the love of Jesus to others and that they in turn will respond in love to those around them.

Today I obeyed the Holy Spirit's nudging. Other days, I refuse to listen and respond. But this particular situation is very dear and close to my heart, and I know that I never want to be the one to stand in the way of Him bringing healing and restoration to other's hearts and lives. Let's pray for each other, that we will learn to listen and obey God's voice so that the towers of discord and strongholds fall down.

# HE'S SINGING OVER ME

One of my most favorite verses is Zephaniah 3:17:

> *The Lord your God is with you, He is mighty to save. He will take great delight in you, He will quiet you with His love, He will rejoice over you with singing.*

I have a very dear friend, Teresa, who sent me a birthday video and she reminded me of this verse and how much God loves me. This is so special to me, as I ponder how God sings over me through the night and gives me peace and joy even during my sleep. I really love it when He wakes me up with a song in the morning that I may not have heard for many years. It reminds me how personal God is to me and how much He really loves me. It brings tears to my eyes just thinking about the goodness of God that I have personally experienced in my life.

I was recently praying for God to help me conduct myself in a way that leads to righteousness, peace, and joy in the Holy Spirit. I looked up Romans 14:17-18, and it says that *anyone who serves Christ in this way is pleasing to God and will be approved by men.*

I can honestly say that my greatest desire is to make God smile and bring Him pleasure from my life, even though I fall short of this so often. I am thankful that He loves me and is willing to help me get back up each time I fall down. He is faithful even when we are not and praise God, His mercies are new every morning.

I can also speak from experience that Proverbs 21:21 (*Those who pursue righteousness and love will find life, prosperity and honor*) has proven true over and over in my life. As I have sought God through every season of my life, I have experienced abundant life, prosperity (not always financially) and honor. It's been one blessing after another. Sometimes the situations did not seem to be a blessing at first, but later I could see God's handprints all over my life.

I pray that you come to personally know the God who desires you, delights in you and sings over you and for dear friends to remind you of this.

# DO NOT WORRY

I have just recently learned that it takes thirty-five days for an eagle egg to hatch. The mother eagle must patiently sit on her eggs, and they are almost never unattended. The males and females take turns patiently sitting on their eggs for the entire thirty-five days.

As I pondered this fact, it made me marvel at our Creator's design and brought up several questions in my mind. If humans had to sit on an egg patiently, would we actually do it? Would we question if it is a real eagle inside? Would we chip away at the shell to see inside? Would both males and females take turns tending to the egg? Would we try to hasten the hatching of the egg? I have often thought it would have been very interesting if a pregnant woman would have a see-through stomach to observe God's handiwork and the process of knitting together a human life. I would suppose this would change how our society views human life at conception. However, God is all-wise, all-knowing and He does all things perfectly without any mistakes.

So often we worry about things and try to take them into our own hands, and we usually end up in a mess. Jesus told us in Matthew 6:25-34 *to not worry, for we are much more valuable than the birds of the air and God takes care of all their needs. Jesus continues to speak of His awesome creation of beautiful flowers which are very temporary and seasonal and yet they do not stress over their existence. He reminds us how much more we can trust ourselves to the care of our Heavenly Father, who knows exactly what we need.* All we must do is seek to please HIM with our lives and He will be completely faithful to handle every care and concern we have.

I pray that as you ponder the God-given instincts of His creation and the spiritual truth of God's word, you will be reminded just how much God loves you and will take care of you and provide for you.

# GO LAY DOWN

Many years ago, I learned to pray when I was missing something because God knows everything.

This happened after I was in an accident on Castleberry Road in Clayton, where the Neuse River is on both sides of the road. I was driving and there were no warning signs up and when I rounded the curve, there was an asphalt roller parked in the road with a man leaning on it holding a stop sign. The speed limit was 45 mph and when I saw this, I began braking, but I honestly thought if he did not move, I would hit him and possibly kill him. Remember, the river was on both sides of the road, so there was no way to go around.

The man realized I was going to crash, and he ran for his life. I hit the asphalt roller head on and totaled my car. I was also six months pregnant.

At the time, my husband worked for the Department of Transportation and knew that they were in violation of the signage rules, so instead of hiring a lawyer, he planned to represent us in court.

When the time came for our court date, even though I am pretty organized, I could not find the file where I would have put it. I knew that our court date was coming up and so I planned to search for it on that Sunday afternoon.

I searched and searched to no avail. I was puzzled and frustrated. What was even more unusual, I kept sensing God was telling me to go lay down and rest. I argued with Him that unless I found the file, I would not be able to rest. I resisted until I had exhausted every corner of my small home.

Very frustrated, I emphatically told God, "Okay, I will rest."

As I was laying my head down, I saw that my husband's closet doors were left open and when I glanced inside, I noticed that the documents and file were placed on the floor of his closet. I could not believe it. I would have NEVER searched there since I would not have put them there. Apparently, he gathered all the information together and put it away in his closet.

As I laid my head down, I was just blown away by the goodness of God instructing me to rest. I resisted His leading, thinking that I knew better and instead of praying about finding them, I pressed on in my own efforts. What a wasted afternoon because of my obstinance.

> *God reveals deep and hidden things, He knows what lies in darkness.*
> *Daniel 2:22*

Since that time, I readily ask God help to help me locate anything that is missing. I am confident He will help me find it in His time and as a result, I have experienced peace in the waiting.

So next time, you misplace something, ask God to help you find it. He will never disappoint you; just remember to trust His timing.

# A LIVING SACRIFICE

Romans 12-1-2 says this:

*Therefore, I urge you, brothers and sisters, in view of God's mercy, to offer your bodies as a living sacrifice, holy and pleasing to God—this is your true and proper worship. Do not conform to the pattern of this world but be transformed by the renewing of your mind. Then you will be able to test and approve what God's will is— His good, pleasing and perfect will.*

Once a candle is lit with fire, it serves its purpose by providing light to guide us in the darkness. It can often provide a sweet fragrance which is pleasing to others. If allowed to burn for a long time, it will be completely used up with no wax or wick left. This is what the Bible is speaking about when it refers to our lives being a living sacrifice. God has given us all specific gifts and abilities to use so we can fulfill His purpose for our lives. When we make God's purpose our main goal in life, we will truly become living sacrifices as God has designed us to be. We only have a short life to live on this earth, so we need to make it count especially since we will meet Him one day when we die.

*We make it our goal to please Him. 2 Corinthians 5:9*

We need to pray and ask God for His direction so that we won't be so busy running around that we actually miss the true purpose of our lives.

Recently, as I pondered what it means to be a living sacrifice, I have prayed for the fire of God to fill me and consume me. What I realized is that there must be an offering for the fire of God to fall. So often, I want all the filling of the Lord in my life, but I refuse to actually surrender my life as an offering to Him to do as He desires with my life. Just like the candle, the wick and wax must be ignited to serve its purpose.

Father, help me to be willing to seek Your will and plans and purposes above my own. For You are good and You have my best interest in mind.

# IT WASN'T ABOUT KARATE

2002 was the year when the earthquake of divorce hit our home. Our home's foundations had been rumbling for many years, and it finally collapsed. I had faithfully prayed for God to restore and redeem our marriage, but obviously when God gives free will to humans, life doesn't always turn out the way we pray.

After our separation, I immediately sought out counseling for my sons, as there was so much pain and anger and rejection swirling around in their hearts. Pastor Lee from Hocutt Baptist Church agreed to meet with my sons, for which I will ever be grateful for his willingness to take the time to lovingly speak truth to my sons.

He not only spent time counseling them weekly at no cost, but he also went way above my request. After meeting with them for a short time, he realized they needed to have a physical outlet for all their pent-up anger and frustrations. He offered to pay for them to take karate lessons because he felt it would be a very positive way for them to vent and release their negative energy.

They began taking the classes and God used this to teach them many valuable lessons. They did not always enjoy it, and often sparring with their opponents brought even more frustrations, but it taught them perseverance, self-control, focus, and keeping their eyes on and obeying their instructor.

They never made it to the black belt level, but I am proud of the endurance it took to complete the level they were on before they finally quit. I will be forever grateful for the investment that Pastor Lee made in their lives.

Titus 2:6-8a says,

> *Encourage the young men to be self-controlled. In everything, set them an example by doing what is good. Your teaching should show integrity, seriousness, and soundness of speech.*

I am sure that one day, God will say to Pastor Lee, "I saw what you did. Well done, good and faithful servant."

You never know when you invest in a child's life how it will impact them and help them to avoid pitfalls and navigate life in a healthy way. Let's be aware of those who may need an encouraging word or deed to help them during hard times in their lives.

# ARE YOU STILL SLEEPING?

**M**atthew 26:40 states,

*Then he returned to his disciples and found them sleeping. "Couldn't you men keep watch with me for one hour?" he asked Peter. When he came back to his disciples, he found them sound asleep.*

This is the question Jesus asked His disciples on the hardest night of His life. He invited His three closest disciples to come with Him to the Garden of Gethsemane to pray after they had eaten His last meal. I believe it would have been an honor for Jesus to single those three men out, and they were chosen because of their close intimacy with Him. Jesus must have wanted fellowship and prayer support as He was facing unimaginable torture. Jesus was/is God, so He must have known that His disciples would fall asleep, not just once but three times, yet He still called them to abide with Him. I cannot fathom the anguish that Jesus felt that night, but I am sure He felt immense stress since the Bible says, *He sweated great drops of blood* (Luke 22:44). From the medical side, I learned that when someone is in extreme stress, capillaries can burst and come out of the pores of your skin.

As I have pondered this, I thought about my own lack of prayer in times when I needed it most, or interceding on behalf of my loved ones, or a friend's prayer concerns. I stand amazed at God's patience with me and my sleepy, complacent ways. Often, when I need Him most to show up, I fail to show up.

Father, please help me to learn how to prevail in prayer and keep from being so distracted from the things that really matter like communicating with the Creator of the universe and Lover of my soul. We have a grand invitation to come boldly as children of God to our Father and lay our requests at His feet. I wonder why I miss so many opportunities to fellowship with Him, the One that knows me best and loves me most.

Father, forgive me and help me to run to You continually with my adoration, my confession of when I miss the mark, my thankfulness for all you have done for me and my prayer for others in need of your intervention.

# A FORGOTTEN DESIRE

I had a wonderful experience when I attended Word of Life Bible Institute, and it truly changed me and the direction of my life. It was there that I decided if I ever had children, I wanted them to have this same wonderful experience at Word of Life and I tucked this in my heart.

Well, I did have two wonderful sons, Benjamin, and John-Mark. I was thrilled to be a mom and had such high aspirations for our family and our sons. However, life can send you lots of surprises and curve balls that you never imagined or thought possible, such as divorce. That was never in my life's plans, but it happened, nonetheless.

During my single parenting years, I forgot about the dreams I had and instead my energy went into survival mode. I began cleaning houses and taking classes to prepare for a career in nursing. The stress was unbearable at times, but God sustained me through it all.

In 2007, we had a wonderful opportunity to go to Word of Life camp in New York for the summer. I worked as a nurse while Benjamin was a lifeguard and John-Mark worked in the dish pit. It was so nice to serve together. I was thrilled that they were able to experience what I had loved so much many years before and my desire for them to attend the Bible Institute began to grow again. I was unsure how that would actually happen though.

After they graduated from high school, they were both given the opportunity to attend the Bible Institute for free from an unlikely source and they both accepted the offer.

It was truly a fulfilled desire of mine for them to experience the Biblical teaching and godly environment which I knew would impact their lives forever.

Psalms 37:4 says:

> *Delight yourself in the Lord, and He will give you the desires of your heart.*

Thank you, Jesus, for blessing us in such amazing ways and helping me to trust you in the hard seasons.

# EXTRAVAGANT GIVER

I am so thankful for all the ways that God provided for me during my years of single parenthood. Both of my sons were involved in the Crosswave Youth Group which was such a blessing all their teen years. The leadership focused on discipling the youth to love and serve Jesus. They modeled this very well and blessed many lives.

One way they served was by coming to our home to rake leaves, wash windows, and paint our shed. Bill, one of the leaders, started a chant to encourage the kids to work as unto the Lord, with "RAKE LEAVES, WASH WINDOWS, PAINT THE SHED." It brought tears to my eyes to experience the love of Jesus in action in my own back yard. I was so encouraged by them helping maintain my home, because at that time, I was extremely busy being a single mom, going to nursing school and cleaning houses.

While they were there, I shared with Bill some of God's extravagant blessings and what amazing ways God had been providing for our family. Bill's response has continued to remain in my mind and heart over the years. He said that he believed one day God would use me to be an extravagant giver to others in need and be able to testify about the faithfulness of God. I have never forgotten those words and believed that God would indeed use me in this way, even though at the time, I felt very dependent and needy.

Today, many years later, I can still visualize those young people working to honor the Lord and bless our home. They worked with excitement and smiles on their faces. I still reflect on the words that Bill said to me and have prayed that I would indeed be an extravagant giver to others.

In 2012, I became a foster parent. In 2015, I served as a nurse for a camp for foster children. In 2016, God led me to begin the REACH Mentoring Ministry for foster youth and other at-risk young people. In 2018, we actually became a non-profit. Since then, we have led events at the children's homes at Falcon and Middlesex. We have collected and distributed countless numbers of hygiene items for foster youth coming into care. We began mentoring clubs in a local high school and elementary school. We secured home furnishings, paid rent, collected money for cars, gathered food items for aged-out foster youth, led day camps for girls, and we are continuing to seek God for direction for new ways to minister and show God's love to these young people.

I know that I have a long way to go to really be an extravagant giver, but this is the desire of my heart to give back to others.

In Luke 12:48, Jesus was speaking to the crowds, and He said,

> *To whom much is given, much will be required.*

This means we are held responsible for what we have. If we have been blessed with talents, wealth, knowledge, time, and the like, it is expected that we are generous to others. I know that I have been blessed beyond measure in my life and I want to share with others who may be going through tough times as well. My goal is to be a conduit of God's love and I hope this inspires you to also be an extravagant giver.

# SHE DID WHAT SHE COULD

I love what my mother-in-love, Edna, shared with me. She heard it in a message she was listening to. Here goes: "Start where you are, use what you have, do what you can and leave the rest to God." This can be a game changer if we really heed the truth of this. As I have pondered this, I remembered so many examples of women in the Bible who did what they could right where they were living. This is all that God really expects of us, that we do our best and give our all for His kingdom purposes. Let's name a few women and what they were able to accomplish by being willing to be pliable clay in the Potter's hands.

Rahab was a prostitute in Jericho, but God gave her an opportunity to change the course of her life when she acknowledged the God of Israel as the one true God, and she saved the lives of the spies that came to her house. As a result, her entire family was spared death (Joshua 2:8-21; 6:22-23).

Esther was a foster girl who lived with her Uncle Mordecai. Through God's providence, she became the Queen of Persia and God used her to save the entire Jewish nation because she was willing to speak up for them at a pivotal time in history (Esther 2-4; 7-9).

The widow Jesus mentioned in Luke 21 gave everything she had to the house of the Lord. She only had two mites, but it was considered more than all the wealthy people gave and Jesus saw her and praised her sacrificial gift.

Mary of Bethany anointed Jesus before His crucifixion with very costly oil. She received criticism from the crowds and even one of

Jesus' disciples, but Jesus recognized her extravagant love and devotion to her Master (John 12:1-8).

Deborah was a woman leader in the time when this was not common in the culture, and she was willing to take a stand when the male leaders were afraid to follow through with God's directions. The battle was won, and she was honored as a Judge for Israel (Judges 4-5).

Ruth was a Moabite who lost her husband early in death. Though she was raised in a pagan culture, she turned to Jehovah and was willing to follow him and care for her mother-in-law with nothing to gain out of it. She willingly worked with diligent hands gathering food and was recognized by Boaz, a kinsman redeemer, who married her. She became the grandmother of King David (Ruth).

Then there were the women who followed after Jesus and helped to care for His needs who did what they were able to support and minister to Jesus.

Dorcas was a woman praised in the community for all her kindness, good deeds and the wonderful clothing she made for others. It might have seemed small to her, but it was meaningful to her friends and neighbors (Acts 9:36-43).

All of these women are an inspiration to my life, and I hope they are for you as well. Let's be women of excellence and remember when we serve others, we are also serving Jesus.

> *Truly I tell you, whatever you did for one of the least of these brothers and sisters of mine, you did for me. Matthew 25:40*

# DO YOU HAVE TERMITES IN YOUR LIFE?

B ack in 2015, I needed to replace the front door of my home. When the repairmen came in the front door, one of the heavier men broke through my floor and we discovered that I had developed termites under my front entrance way. Everything had looked fine from the outward appearance, and I would never have known that I had that destructive process going on until the floor caved in.

I realized that maybe a year earlier, I had the gutters removed and had planned to put up new ones, but I had never followed through with that plan. Also, we had a very rainy season and apparently the rain had leaked in under the house which led to the invasion of the termites.

Thankfully, the damage was limited to just the front entrance to my home, and it was discovered before there was any further damage.

As I pondered the hidden tiny termites in my home, it reminded me of how sin works in our lives. We may allow tiny little things into our lives, and everything continues to look normal from an outward appearance. However, over time, one compromise leads to another and another; then before we realize it, our lives have become broken down and we are not able to hold up under pressure. Ultimately, the foundations of our lives become cracked, and this leads to pain and destruction.

God has some words of warning for us about this from Matthew 7:24-27:

> *Therefore, everyone who hears these words of mine and puts them into practice is like a wise man who built his house on the rock. The rain came down, the streams rose, and the winds blew and beat against that house; yet it did not fall, because it had its foundation on the rock. But everyone who hears these words of mine and does not put them into practice is like a foolish man who built his house on sand. The rain came down, the streams rose, and the winds blew and beat against that house, and it fell with a great crash.*

So, be careful to take inventory of your heart and life. Consider the long-term consequences of your choices. Be a wise person to protect yourself from a slow, hidden erosion of your life's foundation so that you can withstand the storms of life without cracking under pressure.

# DANGER LIES IN THE DARKNESS

A couple of years ago, I had a traumatic experience that reminded me of the movie 'Speed.' Only then, I was in the driver's seat instead of Sandra Bullock driving the bus around and around to prevent a bomb from exploding. I literally kept telling myself that this could not be reality, and yet it was as though I was being controlled and could not stop the course that I was on that day.

I had been under extreme stress both in my personal life and my work life, and apparently this stress caused me to briefly lose my clear judgment. I was at a conference when I received a scam call from the IRS. They threatened me with jail if I hung up and did not cooperate. I am embarrassed to admit that I succumbed to their threats, and I was scammed.

When I finally came to my senses, I was absolutely exhausted from the mental stress that resulted from the time I listened to the lies and deception.

Recently, I was listening to a podcast about what can happen when we remain in the darkness. We have an enemy of our soul, Satan, who does everything in his power to keep us in darkness and isolated so that we cannot hear the voice of truth. Speaking from experience, I am astounded by how we can be deceived when we blindly believe the lies of the enemy. Looking back, if I had prayed or called a friend to advise me during the crisis, this situation would never have happened.

I am learning that when I expose my struggles, they lose power, they shrink in magnitude and God gets bigger. I am then able to stand tall against the enemy waging war against my soul; the light exposes the lies.

The Bible has a solution for this in John 8:12 where Jesus said,

*I am the Light of the world. Whoever follows me will never walk in darkness, but will have the light of life.*

Also, Peter 2:9 states:

*But you are a chosen people, a royal priesthood, a holy nation, a people belonging to God, that you may declare the praises of Him who called you out of darkness into His wonderful light.*

God only has good plans for us, so trust Him as He calls us out of darkness and lies and into truth and light. He loves you so much!

# GOD RESTORES

For many years, I prayed that God would restore my difficult marriage and bring healing to our home. It was a very painful long season, yet I knew that God was and is all powerful and can raise even things that are dead.

Joel 2:25-26 writes this about God,

> *I will repay you for the years the locusts have eaten… You will have plenty to eat, until you are full, and you will praise the name of the LORD your God, who has worked wonders for you; never again will my people be shamed. Then you will know that I am in Israel, that I am the LORD your God, and that there is no other; never again will my people be shamed.*

Now, I felt like my marriage was nearly dead, but I was continually praying and clinging to God's words and His ability to change things around. But finally, after seventeen years of marriage and especially the final seven years of painful intensity, we ended up divorced.

Sometime after I had been divorced, the Lord spoke to my spirit and said, "Susan, I may not have restored your marriage, but I will restore your life." During the next seventeen years, God did just that and has blessed me in unbelievable ways. I would sometimes long to be remarried but I thought to myself that God had already been so good to me, maybe another chance at love and marriage would not be a blessing that I would receive. I had truly become content and at peace and planned to continue to minister with the REACH Mentoring Ministry for foster children.

On May 10, 2017, while I was working at the Johnston County Health Department a patient came in who would forever change my life. He came in for a shot, only because his doctor had run out. Through our conversation, we shared our commitment to the Lord and God must have instantly touched our hearts, because six days later, he asked me for a date.

On our first date, Jay shared that God must be our first priority for a relationship to be successful. These words were like music to my ears, and what I believed in my heart. I knew that I could trust a man ONLY if He trusted and obeyed what God instructs in the Bible. God helped us to see how He had used all the painful circumstances in our lives to draw us close to Jesus and finally to each other.

God continued to unite our hearts until complete culmination on July 6, 2019, when we were united in holy matrimony. God had spoken to Jay during his season of waiting on God that He was going to bless him above anything Jay could have imagined and that our marriage relationship had a bigger purpose than us. So, we have no idea how God is going to use us or what is in our future, but we are so excited for what He has in store for our lives. We truly are *blessed above anything we could have ever imagined* just as Ephesians 3:20-21 states. God has truly restored the years that the locusts have eaten, and we will continue to praise the name of the Lord all the days of our lives for all the wonders He has worked on our behalf.

# GOD'S GRILL

A couple of years ago, I had a white Nissan Altima, and there were some places on it where the paint had chipped away. A kind gentleman offered to touch it up with some paint I had been given by the previous owner, so I assumed it would match my car. Well, the day came for it to be painted; he picked up my car from my work and then brought it back. When I saw it, I was aghast. The white paint did not match, and he drove it back while it was still wet, so the paint had run. It looked horrible! I thanked him, but I knew I would need to get this fixed professionally now, thanks to this freebie.

One day, I was off work and decided to compare prices from paint shops in Smithfield. I went to the first one and the price was definitely more than I had planned to spend on this. I knew there was another shop in Smithfield, but I was unsure where exactly it was. I knew it was either on Market Street or Brightleaf Boulevard, so I did not worry about looking up the exact directions. I drove into Smithfield and turned onto Market Street but did not find it. I went back to Brightleaf Boulevard and drove the entire length of Smithfield and turned around with no success. I finally asked Siri and she gave me the directions. I still missed the entrance because the business had changed names, so I had to drive around the block again. I finally pulled in, parked, and went in to speak with them. He gave me an estimate of $1000.00 for a repair paint job. I then asked him for just the price of the grill since it was the worst part. We went into his office, and he quoted me $300.00 for a new grill. As we were talking, a lady came into his office. He asked her, "What are you doing back so soon?" Apparently, she had just received a new paint job and had just left there. She stated that she had just been in a fender bender and was going to need repairs again.

The owner proceeded to direct me to her car to show me what the new grill would look like. While her car was being evaluated by the owner, another mechanic called me aside and let me know that her car would be repaired, and a new grill would be included in the cost. He said I could have her old one at absolutely no cost to me. All I could say was, "Praise Jesus!" I was just stunned at God's amazing provision once again for me and His impeccable timing. Although I was frustrated at not finding the body shop quickly, God had me in just the right place at just the right time. Had I arrived earlier, this woman would not have been there for me to learn of her misfortune which led to providing a replacement grill for me at no cost.

So, remember, when God says no or makes us wait past the time you think things should have worked out, continue to trust Him! God is never late, but He is always right on time according to His plans and purposes.

Proverbs 3:5-6 says,

> *Trust in the Lord with all your heart and lean not on your own understanding. In ALL your ways acknowledge Him and He will direct your path.*

# A LIFE WELL LIVED

I am so thankful for the Jones family. I met them through their daughter, Amy, who has been a true and faithful friend for many, many years. Her parents Russell and Eva became such a blessing to me and my sons through the years and my life is richer because of their entire family. They have both passed on to Heaven now, but their godly legacy will remain with us forever.

One thing I will always remember and appreciate is that they enjoyed the simple things in life, and they represented Jesus well by their genuine love for others. They freely welcomed us into their family, and we enjoyed many meals on Sunday after church. We relaxed together in the afternoon and read the Sunday newspaper and clipped coupons. They always had a large garden and shared their plenty with us and many others. There was nothing like the Jones' corn harvest either. It was an event with all the family there to help shuck, cook and cut corn for freezing and best of all, eating it. I loved it when we were able to join them for this family event. Many hands make work light, and we loved this wonderful time of fellowship.

It was also so dear to my heart to be claimed as one of their daughters when I went to visit them. They truly cared for me and were always so happy to see me when I stopped by for a visit. They demonstrated this in so many ways, especially when Russell came to my house to install motion cameras after my house was robbed. They were only battery powered, and not hooked up as a security system, but he said they still might discourage people from breaking in. I am so grateful for his concern and investment in our well-being.

They were always interested in how my sons were doing and I am confident they prayed regularly for each one of us. They never were preachy with their beliefs, instead they just lived out a life of faithfulness to Jesus every single day.

Though they have passed on from this life, their memory will never be gone. Psalms 116:15 says,

*Precious in the sight of the LORD is the death of his faithful servants.*

I am sure that Jesus welcomed them, with the words, "Well done, you have been good and faithful servants of mine."

I pray that I will follow their example and live a life well-lived.

# SHAKEN BUT NOT MOVED OR UPROOTED

Recently my husband and I traveled to the mountains of Virginia to visit my son. I was looking forward to the weekend since it was predicted to be peak season for the fall foliage, even though Hurricane Zeta was forecasted to send strong winds our way.

Well, as we neared the mountains, we could see the evidence of the wind as it seemed there was not one pretty leaf left on the trees. They were completely brown and barren except for the evergreens. Of course, I was somewhat disappointed, but God kept speaking to me as we continued to see all the trees stripped of all their leaves, but solidly rooted. Though they had been shaken, they were steadfast and unmovable. One of my favorite verses is I Corinthians 15:58,

> *Be ye steadfast, unmovable, always abounding in the work of the Lord, forasmuch as you know that your labor is not in vain for the Lord.*

Psalms 1 is also a great chapter regarding standing firm when the winds of adversity come. The psalmist describes how we are able to stand firm by delighting in God's words and having our actions align with God's truths. Then we will be like a tree planted by the streams of water, bearing fruit and not withering. Whatever we do will prosper. But the wicked will be blown away like chaff. God promises to watch over the righteous, but the wicked will perish.

As we continue to encounter strong winds of adversity in this year of 2020, hold onto the truth of God's word for dear life and never,

ever let it go. Then when the shaking happens, and it will, you will be still standing even though your leaves might be stripped bare.

# SWEET SHERRY

A true friend is a rare treasure and I have surely been blessed by the Lord with many whom I would consider true friends. Sherry was one of those rare jewels. God thought so as well, for He took her to be with Him way before anyone wanted to let her go.

Sherry and I became friends through church and homeschooling our children. She was creative and always had a smile on her face. She radiated Jesus and always made you feel special and cared for. When she sang in church, she lavishly worshiped Jesus and it showed all over her face. She became a huge conduit of God's love for our family when I became a single mom. She offered to transport my sons to and from school when needed. She would watch them until I got home from nursing classes and send meals home for us. She would take my sons to church or to school activities when I was not able to. Sherry was a prayer warrior and believed in the power of prayer. One time she prayed with me through my home and anointed it with oil. We even prayed and walked around our house seven times, just like Joshua did preparing for the battle of Jericho (Joshua 6).

Over the course of time, Sherry developed cancer. She fought for many years, but eventually her treatment stopped working and she was placed in hospice. I knew visitors were limited during her final days, but one day, I just felt a strong urge to stop by. The nurse let me speak to her husband, Joe, who allowed me to come in. As I was entering, I was told Sherry was actively dying, but her spirit was oh, so alive. She was just like always and asked about me and my sons, instead of herself. She glowed with Jesus, and we were able to pray together. Then I slipped out. She passed later that evening. I am so thankful for God's nudging to visit her at that exact time, and what a precious gift it was to me. I will never forget that big smile on her face.

*Precious in the sight of the Lord is the death of His saints. Psalms 116:15*

I am sure Jesus was right there to welcome her and say, "Well done, good and faithful servant!" (Matthew 25:21)

Thank you, Sherry, for allowing God's love to flow through you and to be an example to all who knew you. I will never forget all your selfless acts of kindness.

# CLAYTON DENTAL OFFICE

We have been with the same dentist for many years. They have watched our sons grow up from toddlers to now grown men. When our family went through a very rough time which happened to be around Christmas, they gave our sons electric toothbrushes to put in their stockings. They have always been very kind and have genuinely cared for us, and still today, my sons both love Mary March. I am so thankful for all of the staff and their support on behalf of our family.

In 2004, a fire burned down the dentist office including all the files and documents. So, at our next appointment, they proceeded to take new x-rays even though they were not due to be taken. When Benjamin's x-ray was reviewed, they discovered there was a growth in his jaw that had actually destroyed some of the bone. The damage was concerning, and we did not know the cause.

This led to the office staff searching to see if they could find any previous x-rays for Benjamin in the rubble that survived the fire. They were successful and actually found his previous one, which did not reveal any growth. This was wonderful as they now had a baseline and could estimate how quickly this had happened. We proceeded with surgical removal and discovered it was just a benign destructive type of cyst. Thank the Lord!

As I have thought about this situation, it overwhelms me at how God works through every hard situation and can bring something good out of it. In this case, without the fire, they would not have taken new x-rays of Benjamin's teeth. This, in turn, could have allowed more permanent and irreparable damage to his jaw. Because he had not been experiencing any discomfort, we would not have had any idea there was a problem. I am so thankful for the fire that led to the discovery that enabled us to preserve Benjamin's health.

It has been many years ago now, but I will never forget how God works through even destructive fires and can bring things to light that have been hidden. Daniel 22:2 says,

> *He reveals deep and hidden things, He knows what lies in darkness and light dwells with Him.*

May this be another reminder that we can trust God no matter what the situation we find ourselves in.

# THE BALLOON RIDE

I had wanted to go on a hot air balloon ride for many years but had never previously had the opportunity. I had heard about a balloon festival coming to Burlington, North Carolina and was excited to make my wish come true. When the time arrived, the weather forecast for the weekend did not look promising. It rained on Friday, so we canceled our plans. On Saturday, the weather cleared up, so we headed for Burlington but by the time we arrived at the festival, it had begun raining again. We were told that no additional flights were available for purchase. I couldn't believe it and was so disappointed.

The balloon pilots still planned for a short flight, but no passengers were allowed to ride. My husband, at the time, went onto the field and started asking the owners if they had room for one person to fly with them and offered them cash. Finally, one of the pilots said that they would be willing to allow me to ride. He accepted the $125 (which was $25 less than the original price) and I was heading out onto the field. The balloon was called the Rainbow Chasers, and it had all the colors of the rainbow on it. They even gave me a disposable camera to take pictures while I was up in the sky which was absolutely stunningly beautiful.

As we were floating along, it was breathtaking and so peaceful. But then it began to lightly sprinkle rain. The pilot made the decision that we would have to come down early to remain safe. As we proceeded with our landing, God sent the most beautiful rainbow in the sky while the sun was setting. It was truly heavenly and reminded me of how much God loves us and how much His promises are true. It also was such a gift that I would never have received without the rain.

On our way home, we stopped by the Christian Life Home and the house parents, Mark and Christy, gave me a beautiful petunia hanging basket. She apologized since it was late for my birthday, but I let her know that she was right on time, since I had just prayed for strong smelling pretty petunias.

This was an amazing day and a wonderful reminder that God loved me and wanted to delight me. God knew I needed this encouragement, and He sent it right on time.

*Delight yourself in the Lord and He will give you the desires of your heart. Psalms 37:4*

# FIT TO BE TIED

Often, I have a difficult time sleeping and when this happens, I feel like God speaks to me about things I maybe need to pray about or give me reminders of His truths that He wants me to know. I think God allows this to happen because I might be too busy to listen and hear His voice during the waking hours.

Anyway, during one of these times, I was reminded of the time I was having devotions with my sons one morning. I don't remember exactly what I was saying, but I spoke about how when we follow Satan's temptations, it will eventually lead to bondage to the very thing that we were tempted with. That day I used a bathrobe tie and tied up their hands as a visual aid. Well, everything was fine, until John-Mark asked me to tie his hands and feet together. After his persistence in asking me, I reluctantly obliged him. We were all sitting on the couch, and it was fun until he started wiggling to get free. Before we realized it, he had fallen off the couch, but because he could not catch himself, he hit his head, and he began having a seizure. I began to panic and immediately called his pediatrician who was located forty-five minutes away. We quickly gathered our things and headed to the doctor.

On my way there, I was pondering how am I going to explain how this happened to the doctor, but fortunately, he was a Christian so hopefully he would appreciate this a little bit. When he came into the room, I began to tell him the story. He looked surprised but supportive and encouraged me to try to teach them a different way next time, which was also my plan. I surely never wanted this to happen again.

As I remembered this situation, it seemed the truth could definitely be learned even more as this could have been very serious. I am thankful that John-Mark did not experience any other issues, but I do hope and pray that the lessons that I strived to teach my sons will not be forgotten, and that God will bring some of these truths back to their minds for the rest of their lives.

*Train up a child in the way he should go, and when he is old, he will not depart from it. Proverbs 22:6*

Sometimes it may not appear that this is true in our children's lives, but I know God's promises are true. In these cases, we as parents must continue to pray for our children that they will return to love and obey the Lord.

# THOSE PEOPLE ARE HURT

I am not sure there is anyone more precious and delightful than my granddaughter. Her name is Abigail Renee. She has bright orange hair, beautiful blue eyes that sparkle, pure white skin, a wonderful, fun personality, and big loving heart. She is two and a half years old right now, but wise beyond her years. She is learning so much every day as a result of her amazing mommy and daddy investing in her life and making her a priority. I am so thankful for their commitment to allow my daughter-in-law Anna to stay home to teach, train and nurture her in the Lord and it is very evident how sensitive Abigail's heart is to things that really matter.

Recently, Anna and Abigail were outside playing, and Abigail heard an ambulance siren. Obviously, she had been taught about what that meant and the importance of praying for them. Well, without any prompting Abigail folded her sweet, little hands and was praying for them in her own little words. Anna was able to capture it on video and you could make out the word, "Amen."

Anna asked her if she heard the siren and Abigail responded, "We need to pray for those people." Anna asked her if she wanted to pray for them and she prayed again with these words, (at least what I could understand), "We need to pray for these people hospital. Amen."

She stood there for a couple more minutes just listening with a concerned look on her face, then said, "Those people are hurt!" and then she walked off to continue playing with her doll.

This is the most beautiful prayer I have ever witnessed from a tiny little girl and if I think so, I cannot imagine how Jesus feels about her heart being so tender and concerned about the hurt people.

I am so thankful Anna was able to capture this on video and share it with me. It truly warms my heart every time I think about it. I have learned so much from Abigail and I am even more diligent in praying for the 'hurt people' every time I hear an ambulance siren.

*Let the little children come to me, and do not hinder them, for the kingdom of heaven belongs to such as these. Matthew 19:14*

# THE COVE

Several years ago, I listened to Pastor Bob from Calvary Chapel because his messages truly ministered to my heart. I heard that he was going to be coming to The Cove for a conference and I really wanted to attend so I called to inquire about the details and cost of the conference.

I honestly had no extra money to spend on this wish of mine, but the registrar told me that they had scholarships available, and I was welcome to apply since I met the qualifications. I practiced the principle of James 4:3 that says,

*We have not because we do not ask God.*

I sent in my application, praying that I would be chosen as one of their recipients and not long afterwards, my prayer was answered. I was so elated that I would be able to attend the conference.

As I drove to Asheville, North Carolina, I praised the Lord the entire way there. I was so grateful for a much-needed retreat to be renewed with God's word. And for the next three days God ministered to my heart and He reminded me how much I am loved.

I continue to be amazed at how God is such an awesome provider and cares about the big and little details of our lives and just wants to bless us. I was so refreshed there by the walking trails lined with Scripture promises, delicious meals, rest, meaningful fellowship with other believers, and the teaching that encouraged and uplifted my spirit.

I'm so thankful for all the ways that God reminds me that I am His princess. He knows me personally and cares about my needs and desires. I hope that you know Jesus as your Heavenly Father. If you don't know Him, just call out to Him in prayer today.

*Cast your cares upon Him for He cares for you. I Peter 5:7*

# YOUR GOD STORY

N ow that you have read some of my God stories, it is time to begin recording your own. May God bless you as you remember and record all His faithfulness, love, provision, and redemption in your own personal life. If you can't think of anything, just ask Him to remind you all the ways He has worked in your life and I'm confident He will answer your request. He loves you so much. and I can't wait for you to begin to recall your account of His lavish love in your life. If you would like to share any of your stories with me, you can email me at susan.stem64@gmail.com. I would love to hear from you.

_____

_____

_____

_____

_____

_____

_____

_____

_____

_____

_____

# ACKNOWLEDGEMENTS

I want to express my gratitude for all of my family, friends, coworkers and even acquaintances who have continually encouraged me through the years to write down my God stories I had shared with them.

My friend, Sylvia, even gave me a short booklet that was entitled, "Write That Devotional Book." I wanted to but struggled with how to begin. My friend, Cindy, encouraged me to turn my God stories into short devotions and her husband, Steve, helped name the book since I use that phrase so often when sharing about God's faithfulness sending one blessing after another (John 1:16).

I am so thankful for my sister-in-law, Andi Stem, who helped me begin the editing process.

A huge thank you to Ruth Griffin, who stepped in to help me complete the editing and publishing of this book. You have been a Godsend, and I am truly grateful to you for all your support and encouragement during the process.

Jim Brown, thank you for your amazing and talented work on the illustration for the cover. I am so thankful you were willing to work with me on this project and especially your ability to capture the image in my head and put it on paper.

Thank you to each of you who will read this book. I pray that God inspires you through this compilation of God's amazing ways and blessings in my life to draw you closer to HIM and help you begin to record all of His faithfulness in your life.

# ABOUT THE AUTHOR

Susan Stem grew up in Ohio in a loving Christian family where she learned to love Jesus. She has always had a heart to minister to outcasts and those who are unloved, and God gave her a dream to have a camp one day where young people would be loved and nurtured. This led her to attend Word of Life Bible Institute where she was able to learn God's word and put it into practice by serving in the youth camps. Upon graduation, she ministered with Youth for Christ in the detention centers and served as a houseparent for the Christian Life Home for pregnant unwed girls.

She has two sons who she homeschooled until she enrolled in nursing school in 2003. She graduated in 2007 and became a foster mom in 2011 after her sons graduated and went off to Word of Life Bible Institute. She volunteered at Royal Family Kids Camp for foster youth as their nurse in 2015 and continued as a volunteer with Teenworks mentoring program.

In 2016, God led her to be the Founder and Director of the REACH Mentoring Ministry for foster and at-risk young people, where she has coordinated and led events at children's homes, began mentoring clubs in the public schools, and has also led summer camps since 2021. She is currently working as a school nurse, which she absolutely loves and provides her ministry opportunities every day. She is continually striving to be a conduit of love to everyone she encounters.

Susan has been happily married to Jay Stem for the past four and a half years. God has truly blessed her with two wonderful sons, Benjamin and John-Mark, daughter-in-law Anna, and a sweet, adorable granddaughter, Abigail, who brings pure delight to her life.

She also loves to read, write, participate, and lead Bible studies, and serve at her church. She enjoys spending time with her family and friends, being adventurous and checking things off on her bucket list.

Most of all, Susan loves Jesus, and is always eager to share all the ways God has lavishly loved and provided for her through the years. She has many more God stories to share and is continuing to write them down for volumes to come.

www.ingramcontent.com/pod-product-compliance
Lightning Source LLC
Chambersburg PA
CBHW071012120626
46546CB00003B/1059